An Evolutionary Theory and Celebration of Male Sexual Arousal by Females

An Evolutionary Theory and Celebration of Male Sexual Arousal by Females

The Foundations of Male Heterosexuality

Marvin Siegelman, Ph.D.

iUniverse, Inc.
New York Lincoln Shanghai

An Evolutionary Theory and Celebration of Male Sexual Arousal by Females
The Foundations of Male Heterosexuality

iUniverse books may be ordered through booksellers or by contacting:

iUniverse
2021 Pine Lake Road, Suite 100
Lincoln, NE 68512
www.iuniverse.com
1-800-Authors (1-800-288-4677)

ISBN-13: 978-0-595-32395-1 (pbk)
ISBN-13: 978-0-595-66549-5 (cloth)
ISBN-13: 978-0-595-77189-9 (ebk)
ISBN-10: 0-595-32395-2 (pbk)
ISBN-10: 0-595-66549-7 (cloth)
ISBN-10: 0-595-77189-0 (ebk)

Printed in the United States of America

I lovingly, adoringly dedicate my book to my precious children Lisa and David, and to my cherished grandchildren Melanie, Elizabeth, Katie, Grace, Samantha, and Henry, who exemplify my quintessential rapture of being alive, my ultimate kvelen and naches!!

Contents

1

Overview.

People say that what we're all seeking is a meaning for life. I don't think that's what we're seeking. I think that what we're seeking is an experience of being alive, so that our life experiences on the purely physical plane will have resonances within our own innermost being and reality, so that we actually feel the rapture of being alive.

—Joseph Campbell (1988, p.3)

This book celebrates the hedonistic rapture of joyous male sexual arousal by, and sexual desire for, lovely females. The most wonderful ecstatic physical excitements that can be experienced, I think, are the delights while looking at, and/or having sex with, a gorgeous, nude female, which typically leads to an approach orientation or desire for this female. This treatise is devoted to understanding the origin, nature, development, and enhancement of the scintillating, magical male rapture of being sexually alive, which remarkably has been almost totally neglected by sexologists (Bancroft, 1987; Janssen, 1995; Regan & Berscheid, 1999; Rosen & Beck, 1988). I operationally define male heterosexuality as the innate capacity and predisposition to be pleasurably sexually *aroused*, automatically, instantaneously, and physiologically (i.e., unconscious neurochemical activation), by the sight of, and sexual interaction with, attractive (i.e., young, healthy, fertile), nude, live females. In our evolutionary past, I believe, males were selected who immediately experienced the *emotion* of pleasurable sexual excitement when they viewed, approached, and had sex with lovely females (Symons 1979, 1995). Males were selected by "mother nature" because their joyous emotional reactions to scintillating females facilitated reproductive success. Hedonism, as reflected in male joy while looking at, and/or physically interacting with, a breathtakingly sexy, nude female, in the service of evolution (i.e., as a necessary precursor that facilitated reproduction), I contend, is not only an innate, automatic, irrepressible, delightful emotional response, it also serves to self-actualize

1

and rejuvenate positive mental and physical health or well-being. I propose that inborn capacities and predispositions that are necessary for the support of life and the enhancement of reproductive success (e.g., arousal to taste of sweet fresh fruit; arousal to sight of attractive nude females) are normal, natural, and beneficial. I contend that males have an inalienable right to indulge their normal dispositions, (and in fact actually do not have any other choice), to enjoy the sight and touch of nude, live, female pulchritude, provided, of course, that *no harm or imposition of any type befalls the female, the responding male, or anyone else.* One of the most important, natural, desirable, and enjoyable raptures of being alive, therefore, is male sexual delight experienced when looking at, and having sex with, a beautiful female. The rapture of being sexually alive for me, (one of many existing raptures of being alive, such as the joys of one's children and grandchildren, the warmth of friendship, being in love, enchantment with music, art, literature, sports, vocation, travel, creativity, discovery, teaching, learning, etc.), has always been embodied and exemplified by the natural and immediate pleasurable excitement that I feel when I look at a ravishing nude, live female, and my thrill is intensified if I am fortunate enough to have sex with this dazzling woman. My exhilarating sexual arousal automatically entices me to continue and to repeat these delightful visual and physical adventures, the more beautiful the female, the more intense my sexual arousal and desire.

Amazingly, there is almost no systematic theory and research on normally functioning heterosexual males concerning the origin, nature, development, and influences (especially on sexual desire) of these singularly crucial male sexual *arousal* responses produced by the sight and touch of lovely, nude, live females (Bancroft, 1987; Janssen, 1995; Regan & Berscheid, 1999; Rosen & Beck, 1988). In human sexuality texts, according to Regan and Berscheid (1999), there is a focus on the physiology of sexual response, for example in the Masters and Johnson (1966) description of physiological reactions to genital stimulation.

> But there is very little mention of sexual desire, the essential spark that ignites the human sexual apparatus that is so precisely detailed. When and if sexual desire is mentioned, it is primarily in discussions of sexual disorders or problems. Why is sexual desire, the center of the whole sexual show, sitting on the sidelines in human sexuality texts? The answer is that there simply isn't much known about it. And there isn't much known about it because early sex research focused on abnormal or pathological sexual phenomenon, on animal sexuality, and on physiological, behavioral sexual events...Comprehensive, explanatory theories that specify causal and antecedent consequences of sexual desire are almost non existent....(Regan & Berscheid, 1999, pp. 1, 2, 28).

The same conclusions can be made about male sexual arousal by females, except even less research has been conducted on male sexual arousal, which I consider to be more crucial than, and actually the major cause of, sexual desire. The research on male sexual arousal has been essentially limited to genital arousal (Rosen & Beck, 1988) and physiological reactions to genital stimulation (Masters & Johnson, 1966). The preponderance of studies in the area of sexual arousal are concerned with evaluating low levels of sexual arousal, typically using genital blood flow measurements (Jansen, 1995; Rosen and Beck, 1988). Male sexual arousal from genital stimulation, according to Masters and Johnson (1966), for example, is associated with increased voluntary-muscle tension, increased heart rate, elevated blood pressure, hyperventilation, voluntary and involuntary muscles contractions, erection, partial elevation of the testes, and elevation and flattening of the scrotal sack. "The definition of sexual arousal…is not easy and it is not surprising that as yet we understand little of its determinants" (Bancroft, 1983, p. 4). The theoretical model presented in this book will focus on pleasurable male sexual arousal by females and will thus omit those male sexual activities that do not involve sexual interaction with females. (e.g., nocturnal penile tumescence, nocturnal emissions, erections during rapid eye movements while asleep, pleasurable genital stimulation with and without erection or orgasm that does not include the fantasy or presence of females, and erection or orgasm resulting from non-sexual causes).

If you are a male, ranging in age from around puberty through old age, who has experienced the raptures of being sexually alive via looking at, and/or having sex with, a lovely female, then you may wonder about why you are turned on, how your body responds (in addition to erection and orgasm), about the development of your excitement, and the important effects of your arousal on your sexual desire. The mission of this book is to present answers to these questions for your consideration. This book, in contrast to all previously published documents that I am aware of, purports to present an original thesis about normal male sexuality that emphasizes male sexual *arousal* in response to *viewing* (but includes the excitement taking place while having sex with), a gorgeous, live, nude female, that includes a *novel* theoretical model of the origin, development, physiology, functions, impact on sexual desire, and significance of this central, paramount, fundamental and necessary pleasurable sexual arousal reaction that occurs while looking at (as well as sexually relating to), appealing females. I seek to *capture the moment* when a male gazes at a blazingly enticing, live, naked female and is delightedly blown away by her rapturously, bewitching and seductive pulchritude. The focus and central construct of my theoretical model is this innate, instantaneous, automatic, in the moment, pleasurable sexual arousal *emotion* that occurs when a typical, normally functioning male *looks at* a lovely, real, live, nude female. I propose that when a male is sexually aroused by a lovely female, this arousal produces a desire to continue looking at, and to again look at, this female, or similarly appealing females. Male sexual arousal and desire are connected in that arousal is primarily responsible for the production of sexual desire, but arousal and desire each have unique and distinguishable qualities and will be discussed separately. I propose that there are two types of pleasurable male sexual arousal to females and two types of male sexual desire for females. In contrast to almost all theoretical models and research concerning sexual desire (Regan & Berscheid, 1999), as well as all theories of personality (Hall, Lindzey & Campbell, 1998) dealing with needs, my approach proposes a theory focused on the emotional reaction of male sexual *arousal*. 1. *Primary innate pleasurable male perceptual sexual arousal by females* is operationally defined as an innate, automatic, in the moment, immediate, predominantly unconscious (i.e., neurochemical, autonomic and somatic activation—see Propositions 4 and 5 in Chapter 2) enjoyable emotional male reaction, starting with intensity around puberty, that occurs when males look at, and/or have sex with, attractive (i.e., young, healthy, fertile), real, live, nude, females, that, under normal conditions, is minimally influenced by factors other than female beauty, and is accompanied with a conscious perception of enjoyment, that may or may not be influenced by factors other than female beauty, such as environmental learning, a state, in the moment experience; and this arousal occurs to a lesser degree when males view graphic representations of nude females. (In an actual real life experience, a male's *conscious* perceptions of his sexual arousal when looking at a real, live nude female could be, and typically is, influenced by cognitions such as his consideration of female caring, sexual excitement, mannerisms, desire to please, look in her eyes, etc., as well as his own sundry attitudes about a particular female. Under controlled conditions, in normally functioning males, however, where male cognitions like those noted in the previous sentence are minimized, male arousals by females, (especially unconscious neurochemical, autonomic and somatic activations), are purported to result predominantly from a male's perception of female physical beauty.) 2. *Primary male sexual desire for females* is operationally defined as an innate, automatic, immediate, conscious male approach disposition starting with intensity around puberty, produced predominantly by primary pleasurable male sexual arousal, that occurs when males look at, and/or have sex with, attractive (i.e., young, healthy, fertile) real, live, nude females, that may or may not be influenced by factors other than female beauty, such as environmental learning, a state, in the moment desire. 3. *Cognitive pleasurable male sexual arousal by females* is operationally defined as an enjoyable emotional male reaction, starting with intensity around puberty, that results from unconscious nerochemical activation, (see Proposition 4 in Chapter 2), that occurs when males think or fantasize about past, present, or future viewing, and/or having sex with, attractive (i.e., young, healthy, fertile) females, but do not actually look at or have sex with an attractive woman, that may or may not be influenced by factors other than female beauty, such as environmental learning, an in the moment state or trait (i.e., ongoing, dispositional) feeling. 4. *Cognitive male sexual desire for females* is operationally defined as a post puberty conscious male approach disposition produced predominantly by cognitice pleasurable male sexual arousal, that occurs when males consciously think or fantasize about past, present, or future viewing, and/or having sex with attractive women, that may or may not be influenced by factors other than female beauty, such as environmental learning, an in the moment state, or an ongoing dispositional trait, of desire. Most studies concerning sexual arousal (Janssen, 1995; Rosen & Beck, 1988), and almost all personality theories (Hall et al., 1998), are concerned with cognitive arousal and cognitive desire. A recent interesting exception reporting on primary sexual arousal is the paper by Janssen, Everaerd, Spiering and J. Janssen (2000), which presents an information processing model of sexual arousal concerning penile reactivity. Whenever male sexual arousal by, and male sexual desire for females is mentioned in this book, *primary* sexual arousal and *primary* sexual desire are referred to, unless otherwise stated.

The central purpose of this treatise is to present a theoretical model that purports to describe and explain the phenomenon of primary pleasurable male sexual arousal by females, and primary male sexual desire for females. I contend that primary pleasurable male sexual *arousal* by females is the most crucial element of male sexuality, which unfortunately has been all but ignored to date. A theoretical model of primary pleasurable male sexual arousal by, and primary male sexual desire for, females is presented in Figure I. In Chapter 2 the literature related to the theoretical model presented in Figure I will be summarized under the following ten propositions: 1: Evolutionary psychology presents the most plausible, and perhaps the only, theoretical approach that explains *why* males are sexually aroused by, and sexually drawn to, young, healthy, fertile females. Proposition 2: Primary pleasurable male sexual arousal by females is conceptualized as a pleasure module. Proposition 3: Primary pleasurable male sexual arousal by attractive females is an experienced positive, momentary, stable, predominantly unconscious, emotional state. Proposition 4: When appropriate emotion elicitors are perceived when males see and/or have sex with attractive females, dedicated neurochemical substrates are activated that prepare action dispositions to continue and to repeat the experienced pleasurable sexual arousal. Proposition 5: Primary pleasurable male sexual arousal by nude females is expressed through autonomic reactions, somatic and behavioral expressions, and self-perceptions of pleasurable sexual arousal that reflects the preparation and action dispositions to continue and to repeat these experienced pleasures. Proposition 6: The sexual joy experienced when a male views and/or has sex with a lovely female serves as the core reinforcement of his approach orientation towards females. Proposition 7: The visual perception of different levels of real, live, nude female attractiveness observed by males is the principal determinant of different levels of primary pleasurable male sexual arousal and by females. Proposition 8: Primary male sexual desire for attractive females is an in the moment, conscious, cognitive approach disposition resulting mainly from primary pleasurable male sexual arousal by attractive females. Proposition 9: Different levels of real, live, nude female attractiveness observed by males are the essential determinants of different levels of primary male sexual desire for females. Proposition 10: The trait of male pleasurable arousal capacity, male personality traits, and male situational appraisal could influence pleasurable male sexual arousal by, and male sexual desire for, females.

Figure I. Theoretical Model of Primary Pleasurable Male Sexual Arousal by Females.

Origin and Process of Primary Pleasurable Male Sexual Arousal by Females.

1. Evolutionary psychology.   (Proposition 1)

2. A pleasure module.   (Proposition 2)

Structure of Primary Pleasurable Male Sexual Arousal by Females

1. A positive, in the moment, stable, mainly unconscious, emotional state.   (Proposition 3)

2. Dedicated neurochemical substrates.   (Proposition 4)

3. Autonomic, somatic, behavioral, and self-perception reactions.   (Proposition 5)

Goal of Primary Pleasurable Male Sexual Arousal by Females.

1. Reinforcement of approach orientation toward females.   (Proposition 6)

Immediate Determination of Level of Primary Pleasurable Male Sexual Arousal by Females.

1. Level of female attractiveness.   (Proposition 7)

Structure and Immediate Determination of Primary Male Sexual Desire for Females.

1. An in the moment, conscious, cognitive wish produced predominantly by   (Proposition 8)
primary pleasurable male sexual arousal by females, but more variable than
arousal.

2. Level of female attractiveness.   (Proposition 9)

Male Arousal Capacity, Male Personality Traits and Male Situational Appraisal Influences on Primary Pleasurable Male Sexual Arousal by Females and Primary Male Sexual Desire for Females.

1. Male arousal capacity trait.   (Proposition 10)

2. Male personality traits.

3. Male situational appraisal.   (Proposition 10)

A major reason for the paucity of research on male sexual arousal in response to different levels of female attractiveness is that no measurement of this type of arousal exists. A structure for such an instrument will be presented in Chapter 3 in Proposition 11, within a research design for testing the evolutionary predictions that males are most aroused sexually by young, healthy, fertile nude females, and stressing the *construct validity* (Cronbach & Meehl, 1955) of these arousal instruments. On the basis of theoretical assumptions underlying the nature of pleasurable male sexual arousal (i.e., neurochemical, autonomic, somatic, behavioral, and subjective feelings described in Propositions 4 and 5 below in Chapter 2), and the qualities of female attractiveness (i.e., youth and health), criteria will be presented for the construction of male sexual arousal measures and female attractiveness evaluation. In addition, designs for the construction of male sexual desire for female instruments will be outlined in Chapter 3 in Proposition 11. Proposition 11: Research methodology, including the measurement of primary pleasurable male sexual arousal by females and primary male sexual desire for females, is required to test hypotheses derived from evolutionary theory that emphasizes the construct validity of these male sexual arousal and desire measurements.

The position is taken that male sexual arousal by attractive (i.e., young, healthy, fertile) females is a universal, innate, spontaneous, automatic, intractable and unique evolutionary adaptation that facilitated gene transmission by serving as a foundation and necessary component of male sexual desire for these females.

The proposal is made that heterosexual males, from puberty through old age, have an innate capacity and predisposition to instantaneously *respond* with different degrees of pleasurable sexual *arousal* when they look at, and/or interact sexually with, real, live, nude females representing different levels of female attractiveness (i.e., age and health indicating level of fertility). The highest levels of sexual excitement occur in response to the view of the healthiest females between the ages of 15 and 18, who represent the highest levels of fertility. Pleasurable male sexual arousal appears to reinforce the acts of looking at, and interacting with, attractive females, which produces a *desire* to continue and to repeat the enjoyment of seeing and relating to young, healthy, fertile females. The speculation is made that pleasurable *visual* arousal is primary and necessary in producing a male's desire to not only see, but to sexually interact with, the perceived attractive female, an expression of an approach orientation. Male sexual arousal is proposed to be an *emotion* consisting of neurochemical, autonomic, somatic, behavioral, and subjective self-perceptions of excitement components (in this descending order of automaticity and progression from unconscious to conscious levels). Primary pleasurable male sexual arousal and primary male sexual desire are considered to be an in the moment, immediate response *state* to a particular female. An additional premise of this paper is that male sexual arousal to the view of, and interaction with, nude females are visual and kinesthetic sensory functions analogous to taste, hearing, and smell. Enjoying the sight and touch of a lovely female is comparable to the evolutionary adaptation of enjoying the taste of sweet, fresh fruit, except the visual turn on is unique to males. When we taste delicious sweet food, we experience a pleasurable arousal to this sweet taste and immediately have a desire to continue eating, and to eat again, this sweet food, or an equally tasty sweet food. When we see, and or have sex with, an attractive nude female, we are pleasurably aroused sexually and immediately have a desire to continue looking at, to continue having sex with, and to repeat these pleasures with that female or a similarly captivating female. I propose that we are not born with a desire to eat sweet tasty food (a desire to see and have sex with attractive females), but rather that we are born with an innate *capacity* and predisposition to *respond* immediately with gustatory enjoyment when we eat sweet savory food (respond with pleasure when seeing and/or having sex with appealing females), and an innate capacity and inclination to instantly respond with a desire to continue eating and to again eat that flavorful sweet food (desire to continue seeing and/or to continue having sex with, and to see again, and to again have sex with, that lovely female). Male sexual arousal, especially the essential and critically vital *visual* arousal, is considered to be the foundation and most important unifying and directional force in male sexuality, and as potent a motivator as the pleasure of eating delicious food. "Telling men not to become aroused by signs of youth and health is like telling them not to experience sugar as sweet" (Buss, 1994, p. 71). I consider pleasurable male sexual excitement that occurs while looking at a ravishing nude female to be the primary, most potent, and perhaps the only true male *aphrodisiac*, the ultimate "libido" source of male sexuality. For me, sexual arousal in response to the *view* of lovely nude females has always ignited my sexual desire for these females, represents a remarkable, omnipresent, and glorious example of the "rapture of being alive" (Campbell, 1988), and when coupled with orgasmic arousal delights, becomes my quintessential celebration of sexual joy.

Although there are no studies to date that directly and specifically evaluate the evolutionary prediction that males respond with different levels of emotional sexual arousal to females varying in attractiveness (i.e., age, health, and fertility), wherein this emotional response includes neurochemical, autonomic, somatic, behavioral, and subjective self-perceptions of excitement components, there is a considerable body of literature that is relevant to, and generally supportive of, these predictions. The relevant literature concerning these predictions is summarized and discussed in Chapter 2. Research methodology to evaluate these predictions will be presented in Chapter 3. Chapter 4 will include a conceptual framework of male sexual arousal by, and desire for females, basic assumptions, major principles and a discussion of puberty and adolescence, the critical period, I believe, for the formation of male sexuality. Chapter 5 will present several implications and predictions based on the assumptions and principles outlined in Chapter 4. A general conceptual framework of emotional hedonic arousal and cognitive desire applicable to males and females will be described in Chapter 6. Chapter 6 will continue with proposals for the relationship between innate male sexual arousal by females and non-sexual behavior, including morality, identity and autonomy, prejudice and personality. Finally, Chapter 6 will conclude with a look ahead to new directions.

This book is a validation and celebration of male sexual arousal by females, recognizing the monumental importance of male sexual arousal for all humans passed, present and future, and a rejoicing in this spectacularly ecstatic experience. I believe that this book will convey a convincing message, based on sound theoretical principles and supported by cutting edge research evidence, that male sexual arousal that occurs when a male looks at an attractive live, nude female, reflects an evolutionary adaptation, is an innate, automatic, universal, physiologically-based, emotional response that is a necessary part of male sexuality to be totally accepted, nourished, and celebrated.

2

A Theoretical Model of Male Sexual Arousal by Females.

PROPOSITION 1: EVOLUTIONARY PSYCHOLOGY PRESENTS THE MOST PLAUSIBLE, AND PERHAPS THE ONLY, THEORETICAL APPROACH THAT EXPLAINS *WHY* MALES ARE SEXUALLY AROUSED BY, AND SEXUALLY DRAWN TO, YOUNG, HEALTHY, FERTILE FEMALES.

Evolutionary psychology is psychology informed by the fact that the inherited architecture of the human mind is the product of the evolutionary process (Cosmedes, et al., p. 7). A central tenet of evolutionary psychology is that the human brain has necessarily been shaped by natural selection and that mental adaptations exist just as anatomical and physiological ones do. Specifically, the human brain contains cognitive/emotional mechanisms, often referred to as *psychological mechanisms* shaped by natural selection. These complex mechanisms presumably evolved in response to specific adaptive problems early hominids encountered in the Pleistocene (Buss, 1991, 1994; Tooby & Cosmides, 1992). One may think of psychological mechanisms as information-processing programs which have evolved as a result of natural selection...evolutionary theorists posit that contemporary men and women possess specific psychological mechanisms (which may or may not be currently adaptive) that were selected because they were adaptive-at least to some degree-during the longest period of human evolution-the environment of evolutionary adaptiveness (EEA). In other words, some of the most apparent psychological mechanisms may have to do with the process of mate attraction, selection and retention, sexual arousal, and so on (Buss & Schmitt, 1993; Symons, 1979, 1992) (Allgeier & Wiederman, 1994, pp. 221,231).

A male psychological mechanism that evolved from our ancient male ancestors that facilitated reproductive success, postulated in this book, is that males are born with the capacity and predisposition to experience the emotion of pleasurable sexual arousal when they see, and/or have sexual contact, especially sexual intercourse, with attractive (i.e., young, healthy, fertile) nude, live females. Our ancient male ancestors were selected because they had the capacity and predisposition to be aroused by, and thus drawn to, as well as enjoy sex with, young, healthy, fertile, females, producing the greatest reproductive success, an adaptation that facilitated gene transmission. I would speculate that when these selected males were sexually aroused, subjectively and physiologically, by the *view* of an attractive, nude female, their visual arousal immediately triggered a sexual desire to interact physically with that female, and when they did, they found sexual intercourse, especially orgasm resulting from intercourse, to be very pleasurable, which in turn immediately produced and intensified their desire to continue and to repeat looking at and having sex with that female, as well as other similarly attractive females. The enjoyable arousal experienced by males today when they look at and have sex with such appealing females, produces and reinforces the desire to continue, and to repeat, these exciting experiences. I am proposing that males are *not* born with a desire to look at and to have sex with attractive females. Males are born with the capacity and predisposition to *respond* with pleasurable excitement when they see and/or have sex with attractive females, which activates and reinforces his innate capacity and inclination to *continue* and to *repeat* the pleasures of looking at, and having sex with, an attractive female, or with similarly attractive females, which constitutes his sexual *desire* for these females.

The proposal is made that the emotional experience of pleasurable male sexual arousal when viewing and/or interacting with attractive nude females, (i.e., a male psychological mechanism), is part of human nature or innate. From an evolutionary biology perspective, three criteria are described by Buss (1984) which determine whether or not an attribute, such as a psychological mechanism, is part of human nature and an important species typical characteristic. The first criterion is *universality*. "Features found across cultures, races, and populations are assumed to be more part of human nature than those features that are unique to certain subgroups or individuals…" (Buss, 1984, p. 1138). Cross-cultural studies that found female youth and attractiveness, signaling reproductive capacity, to be valued by males in selecting short-term and long-term mates (Buss, 1989, 1990), and cross-cultural investigations that reported that males find female attractive-ness to decline with increasing female age (Jones, 1995; Kenrick & Keith, 1992), tend to support the universal predisposition of males to respond positively to young, healthy females. Considerable agreement in the judgment of female facial attractiveness as representing youthfulness and health in cross-cultural studies (Cunningham, Roberts, Barbie, Druen & Wu, 1995; Jones, 1995; Langlois & Roggman, 1990; Langlois, Kalanknis, Rubenstein, Larson, Hallam & Smoot, 2000) also supports universal tendencies for male consistency and similarity in evaluating female beauty in terms of youth, health, and fertility. In all of the above studies of mate choice, preferred female age and agreement on female facial characteristics, it should be noted, that male sexual *desire* was evaluated or implied but male sexual *arousal* was not measured or referred to.

A second criterion suggested by Buss (1984) to evaluate the inclusion of an attribute as part of human nature is *spontaneity, automaticity,* and *intractability.* These three qualities are, "…produced spontaneously with little or no environ-mental impetus or incentive…. reflexively displayed in response to a given envi-ronmental elicitor…difficult to alter…" (Buss, 1984, p. 1139). The ubiquitous, intense, historical male preoccupation with female erotica and pornography (Peterson, 1999; Symons, 1979), prostitution (Bullough, 1964, 1996), promis-cuity (Kinsey, Pomeroy, & Martin, 1948; Symons, 1979), and polygamy (Buss, 1994; Daley & Wilson, 1983; Kinsey et al.; Symons, 1979) attest to the indomi-table, unparalleled male arousal response to, and pursuit of sexual excitement with young, healthy females, especially in response to, and pursuit of, a *variety* of female encounters (Symons, 1979), despite enormous and persistent societal efforts to curb these proclivities (Peterson, 1999; Symons,1979). Male arousal by, and desire for, pornography, prostitution, promiscuity, and polygamy appear to reflect spontaneous, automatic, and intractable male proclivities. As noted above, (but worth repeating), Buss (1994) concluded that telling men not to become aroused by signs of youth and health is analogous to telling them not to experi-ence sugar as sweet.

The third criteria presented by Buss (1984) for the determination of whether or not a characteristic is an important species-typical attribute is *adaptation,* described as, "species features that solve ecological problems and enable organ-isms to function well in their niches…" Buss, 1984, p 1139). Symons (1979) writes that a male adaptation was to find young, healthy women to be physically attractive because these women were the most fertile and so had the greatest reproductive value. "Because a male can potentially impregnate a female at almost no cost to himself in terms of time and energy, selection favored the basic male tendency to become sexually aroused by the sight of females..." (Symons, 1979, p. 80). Males who were sexually aroused by the sight of females and the female genitals, according to Symons (1979), were so consistently favored by selection that such arousal became innate. The male adaptation to find young, healthy females sexually arousing and desirable, as this proclivity facilitated reproductive success in our ancient forefathers, certainly appears to be a fundamental and important species-typical attribute.

> Carl Gustav Jung (1953–1978) saw personality as the product of ancestral history. Jung, more than any other psychologist, has probed into man's history to learn what he can of the racial origins and evolution of personality. Modern man has been shaped and molded into his present form by the cumulative experiences of past generations extending far back into the dim and unknown origins of man as a separate species. The collective unconscious is the psychic residue of man's evolutionary development, a residue that accumulates as a consequence of repeated experiences over many generations. Racial memories or representations are not inherited as such; rather we inherited the possibility of reviving experiences of past generations. They are predispositions which set us to react to the world in a selective fashion. These latent or potential memories depend upon inherited structures and pathways that have been engraved on the brain as a result of the cumulative experiences of mankind (Hall & Lindsey, 1957, pp. 79–81).

One major disagreement that I have with Jung is that male ancestral history is unique or qualitatively different from female ancestral history. Specifically, male pleasurable intense sexual arousal to nude female physical beauty, determined by his evolved ancestral history, is unique. I propose that females do not have an equivalent intense pleasurable sexual arousal to nude male physical beauty that is determined by their ancestral history.

An interesting recent genetic finding is that the Y chromosome, studied by DNA analysis, is paternally inherited, where human males have one Y chromosome and one X chromosome, and females have two X chromosomes (Bradman & Thomas, 1998; Jobling & Tyler-Smith, 1995). The Y chromosome that a father passes to his son is, in large measure, an unchanged copy of his own Y chromosome, and has been traced back as far as 400,000 years (Bradman & Thomas, 1998). Could the Y chromosome contain genetic DNA responsible for the male innate predisposition to be sexually aroused by a lovely nude female?

PROPOSITION 2: PRIMARY MALE SEXUAL AROUSAL BY FEMALES IS CONCEPTUALIZED AS A PLEASURE MODULE.

Primary male sexual arousal is conceptualized as a *pleasure module* analogous to the "fear module" depicted by Öhman and Mineka (2001). From an evolutionary perspective, Öhman and Mineka (2001) describe four characteristics of an evolved central motive state of fear, depicted as a "fear module," as (1) selectivity, (2) auatomaticity, and (3) encapsulation, based on (4) dedicated neural circuitry, that motivated avoidance and escape in our ancient ancestors when they were faced with dangers that threatened their survival. In reference to selectivity, Öhman and Mineka (2001) state that, "rather than being open to any stimulus, the fear module is assumed to be particularly sensitive to stimuli that have been correlated with threatening encounters in the evolutionary past" (p., 485). These fear relevant stimuli directly and automatically activate the fear module, which is not under voluntary control, in order to facilitate, "...efficient attention capture..." (Öhman & Mineka, 2001, p. 485). Concerning encapsulation, "...once activated, a module tends to run its course with few possibilities for other processes to interfere with or stop it. In particular, evolutionary shaped modules will be resistant to conscious cognitive influences because their origin typically precedes recent evolutionary events, such as the emergence of conscious thought and language" (Öhman & Mineka, 2001, p. 485). The fourth characteristic of the fear module posited by these authors is that the fear module originates in a dedicated or specific neural circuitry center in the amygdala. "...automaticity is primarily related to the initiating of activity whereas encapsulation refers more to the maintaining of activity over time" (Öhman & Mineka, 2001, p. 485). The fear module qualities of selectivity, automaticity and encapsulation described by Öhman and Mineka (2001) are quite similar to the three characteristics that Buss (1984) considered to be critical for the determination of whether or not a characteristic was part of human nature, or a species-typical attribute, namely spontaneity, automaticity, and intractability (described above in Proposition 1). Pleasurable male sexual arousal to attractive females, then, is considered to be an evolved central motive state of pleasure, depicted as a *pleasure module*, that motivated approach toward females in our ancient male ancestors when they were faced with the problem of passing their genes on to subsequent generations. Our ancient forefathers responded with sexual bliss, in a selective/spontaneous, automatic, encapsulated/intractable manner, that was resistant to conscious cognitive influences, on the basis of dedicated neurochemical substrates, when they looked at and/or had sex, especially sexual intercourse, with attractive, young, healthy females (Buss, 1984; Öhman & Mineka, 2001).

PROPOSITION 3: PRIMARY PLEASURABLE MALE SEXUAL AROUSAL BY ATTRACTIVE FEMALES IS AN EXPERIENCED POSITIVE, IN THE MOMENT, STABLE, PREDOMINANTLY UNCONSCIOUS, EMOTIONAL STATE.

Primary pleasurable male sexual arousal by females involves capturing an emotional moment in time, a moment that males want to extend and repeat again. This captured moment is embodied in the concepts of "instant utility" (Kahneman, 1999) and "instantaneous utility" (Shizgal, 1999). In his discussion of objective happiness, Kahneman (1999) presents a useful description of an attribute called "instant utility," borrowing the term "utility" from Bentham (17 89/1948). "Being pleased or distressed is an attribute of experience at a particular moment" (Kahneman, 1999, p. 4), which is labeled instant utility, is evaluated as, "Good/Bad," and is, "...best understood as the strength of the disposition to continue or to interrupt the current experience" (Kahneman, 1999, p. 4). Shizgal (1999) incorporates instant utility (Kahneman, 1999) in his concept of "instantaneous utility" and adds a bias of the subject, "...to repeat actions that have led to pleasant consequences in the past" (p. 502), which is essentially the *law of effect* (Thorndike, 1932). Primary pleasurable male sexual arousal is proposed to be a *state reaction* that occurs at a specific time in response to a particular female, is characterized as "instantaneous utility" (Shizgal, 1999), and proposes to "capture the moment." Primary male sexual arousal thus includes pleasurable sexual arousal *while viewing* a real, live nude female (Okami & Shakelford, 2001), with the concomitant bias to continue this pleasurable experience, and the disposition to repeat this sexual pleasure, an approach orientation (Zajonc, 1998), the foundation or preparation of male sexual desire for females. Sexual arousal and desire for females can occur, of course, when not in the presence of a real, live nude female, as when looking at graphic representations of females (i.e., primary male sexual arousal and desire), and via imagery, literature, verbal descriptions, etc.

(i.e., cognitive male sexual arousal and desire). The cognitive forms of sexual arousal and desire are considered to be dispositional, ongoing, continuous *traits* and are *estimates* of immediate, in the moment arousal and desire (i.e., instantaneous utility or primary arousal and desire) but they can be used for research purposes, but they are not ideal representations of male sexual arousal and desire. Sexual arousal is an in the moment *emotional* response.

> In fact it can be readily argued that of all major psychological processes, the emotions are of prime importance. For a world bereft of emotions can not exist or be imagined. Could there be affiliation, could there be friendship, or art, or mating, or reproduction, or for that matter, could there be life? Take classical conditioning. In order for conditioning to occur a response must previously be succeeded by a reinforcing event. And an event is reinforcing only if the organism can discriminate it as a positive or a negative event. No learning and performance could emerge or be sustained because there would be no incentives, for incentives exist only by virtue of their positive or negative consequences (Zajonc, 1998, p. 591).

"The affect system has been sculpted by the hammer and chisel of adaptation and natural selection to differentiate hostile from hospitable stimuli and to respond accordingly" (Cacioppo, Gardner & Berntson 1999, p. 840). "Emotional capacities may exemplify human universals of mind and represent experiences closer to the genes than observable behavior" (Symons, 1979, p. 46). The conceptual model concerning emotion presented by Lang (1994, 1995) will serve as the structural and functional framework of primary pleasurable male sexual arousal by females.

> Emotions are products of a Darwinian development and could be characterized as motivationally tuned states of readiness....Emotions are action dispositions....driven by only two opponent motivational systems appetitive and aversive—subcortical circuits that mediate reactions to primary reinforcers. Emotions are about doing something that is important to the organism (escape, attack, sexual consummation, etc.,)....on the other hand, curiously, the defining acts may or may not actually occur...emotions quintessentially occur in a behavioral hiatus, as states "experienced," then reported on and evaluated....It is in this sense that they are dispositions and not the acts themselves: They reflect central activation and preparation for action....affects are driven by two primary motive systems: the appetitive system (consummatory, sexual, and nurturant), prototypically expressed by behavioral approach, and the aversive system (protective, withdrawing, and defensive), prototypically

expressed by behavioral escape and avoidance….it is proposed that two motive systems exist in the brain—appetitive and aversive—accounting for the primacy of the valence dimension. Arousal is not viewed as having a separate substrate, but rather as reflecting variations in the activation (metabolic and neural) of either or both systems…(Lang, 1995, pp. 372–374).

The dimension of pleasant/unpleasant, first introduced in this country by Titchner (1908), and level of activation (i.e., arousal) have been found consistently across studies (Lang, 1994, 1995; Smith & Ellsworth, 1985; Zajonc, 1998). Most theories of emotion assume that emotions are primarily adaptive in an evolutionary sense (Darwin, 1873/1965; Hamburg, 1963; Izard, 1989; Nesse, 1990; Smith & Ellsworth, 1987). Davidson (2000b) points out a diverse body of literature (Cacioppo & Gardner, 1999; Davidson & Irwin, 1999b; Gray, 1994; Lang, Bradley & Cuthbert, 1990; Schnierla, 1959; Watson, Wiese, Vaidya & Tellegen, 1999), converging on the idea of two fundamental systems that underlie approach and withdrawal related emotion and motivation, or certain types of positive and negative affect. "It would indeed be surprising if the valence dimension did not dominate the dimensional structure of emotion. To the extent that the emotions serve the adaptive function and allow the individual to draw on the resources of the environment and protect the individual from its dangers, the approach avoidance dichotomy is all-important" (Zajonc, 1998, p. 608). Primary pleasurable male sexual arousal is postulated to be one type of positive affect that fosters and predisposes males to approach attractive females. (See Zajonc, 1998 for an excellent in-depth review and analysis of emotions.)

PROPOSITION 4: WHEN APPROPRIATE EMOTION ELICITORS ARE PERCEIVED WHEN MALES SEE AND/OR HAVE SEX WITH ATTRACTIVE FEMALES, DEDICATED NEUROCHEMICAL SUBSTRATES ARE ACTIVATED THAT PREPARE ACTION DISPOSITIONS IN MALES TO CONTINUE AND TO REPEAT THE

EXPERIENCED PLEASURABLE SEXUAL AROUSAL BY FEMALES.

The perceptual processing of appropriate emotion elicitors in male sexual arousal involves the identity, location, and the physical properties (Shizgal, 1999) of visual cues (i.e., nude females) and somesthetic cues (i.e., penile-vaginal intercourse). The pleasurable emotional experience, an "instantaneous utility" (Shizgal, 1999), of male sexual arousal occurs only when these spontaneous and selected (Buss, 1984; Öhman & Mineka, 2001) visual and somesthetic cues are perceived. This requirement follows the "diathesis" model of Davidson (1992a), which holds that anterior prefrontal cortex (PFC) activation predisposes a person to respond with positive or negative affect only when, "...given an appropriate emotion-elicitor" (p. 129).

The conscious perception of emotion-elicitors (e.g., view of nude female), and the conscious perception of emotional feelings (e.g., self-reports of sexual arousal) are implemented by different neural circuitry than the production of emotional reactions or feelings (Davidson & Tomarken, 1989; Davidson, 1993; Ito & Cacioppo, 1999; Tomarken & Keener, 1998), such as male conscious perception of sexual arousal. The perceptual processing that occurs when looking at a nude female, the self-reports of pleasurable sexual feelings, and the conscious desire to see and have sex with this attractive female, have different neurochemical substrate than the neurochemical substrates that are unconsciously activated during pleasurable emotional experiences (Davidson, 1992a, 1993; LeDoux, 1999). These unconscious neurochemical reactive processes that are the foundation of emotional experiences including male sexual arousal by females are considered next.

For Carl Lange (18 85/1922), "...emotion *was* its physiology..." (Lang, 1994, p. 212). An emotion network, according to Lang (1993), would include connections to sub-cortical motivation circuits, mediating response programs for visceral mobilization, and approach or defense. "These connections to 'hard-wired' reflex systems lend a network coherence and may account for their persistence, for example, as in...the idiosyncratic patterns of sexual arousal" (Lang, 1994, p. 219). There is abundant evidence that emotions occur without conscious cognitions (Damasio, 1999; Dimberg, Elmehed & Thumberg, 2000; Izard, 1984, 1989, 1993; LeDoux, 1992, 1993, 1995, 1996, 2000; Rosen & Schulkin, 1998; Zajonc, 1980, 1984, 1998). Zajonc (1984), for example, presents and reviews convincing evidence that, "untransformed pure sensory inputs directly generate emotional reactions" (p. 122).

I propose that male sexual arousal by attractive females is associated with, and probably produced by, unconscious, "hard-wired," neurochemical substrate, including: (a) increased activation of the left prefrontal cortex (Davidson, 1984, 1992a, 1994, 1998a; Davidson & Fox, 1982, 1989a; Tomarken & Keener, 1998); (b) left PFC activation increase of recovery time (Davidson, 1998a), (c) slow cortical response indicated by positive-going slow waves (Cuthbert, Schupp, Bradley, Birbaumer & Lang, 2000; Lang, Bradley & Cuthbert, 1998); (d) the release of dopamine (Bancroft, 1999, 2002; Berenbaum, Raghaven, Le, Vernon & Gomez, 1999; Berridge, 1999; Depue, Luciana, Arbisi, Collins & Leon, 1994; Depue & Collins, 1999; Hoebel, Rada & Pothos, 1999; Wise, 1996; Zuckerman, 1991); (e) activation of the nucleus accumbens (NAc) extension of the amygdala (Hoebel et al., 1999; Grant, et al., 1996; Koch, Schmid & Schlnitzler, 1996; Lang, et al., 1998; Volkow, Wang & Fowler, 1997); (f) left PFC glucose metabolism (Abercrombie et al., 1996; Sutton et al., 1997); (g) left amygdala cerebral blood flow (Ketter et al.); (h) testosterone levels and release (Bancroft, 1989, 2002; Regan & Berscheid, 1999, Zuckerman, 1991). The seminal research of Davidson and his colleagues (1992a, 1993, 1998a; Davidson, Jackson & Kalin, 2000; Davidson, Pizzagalli, Nitschke & Putnam, 2002) during the past two decades on electroencephalographic (EEG) asymmetric prefrontal cortex (PFC) activity, presents substantial evidence that positive emotional approach behavior is associated with left PFC activation, and that negative emotional withdrawal behavior is related to right sided PFC activation. Ekman, Davidson and Friesen (1990), for example, found that while participants viewed positive film clips they exhibited *Duchenne smiles*, purported to be associated with the spontaneous occurrence of enjoyment, and had elevated levels of left PFC activation. Left PFC activation also increases recovery time (i.e., time course) by maintaining representation of behavioral reinforcement contingencies (i.e., behavioral approach), according to Davidson (1998a). A scalp-recorded EEG response that evaluates the arousal intensity or activation of an emotional reaction, irrespective of the affective valence (pleasure-displeasure), is the late, slow positive voltage change that is significantly larger for affective than for neutral stimuli (Cuthbert, et al.). The slow positive voltage change was increased for erotic pictures that prompted accentuated autonomic (i.e., heart rate and skin conductance) responses, emotional facial expressions, and self-reports of greater affective arousal, which led to the conclusion that, "...the late positive wave indicates a selective processing of emotional stimuli, reflecting the activation of motivational systems in the brain" (Cuthbert, et al., p. 95). The prediction is made that left PFC activation, left PFC recovery time (Davidson, 1998a) and slow cortical voltage change (Cuthbert et al.) in males, will be associated with male perception of different levels of nude female attractiveness; the more attractive the female, the higher the left PFC activation (i.e., lower left PFC alpha power), the longer the recovery time, and the greater the positive increase in slow cortical voltage in male reactivity.

There is robust support indicating that dopamine is associated with positive affect (Berenbaum et al., 1999; Depue et al., 1994; Hoebel et al., 1999; Wise, 1996). Dopomine neurons seem to be crucial in the causal events accountable for rewarding and motivational effects of hypothalamic stimulation (Hoebel, 1988; Valenstein, 1976; Wise, 1996; Yeomans, 1989). Sexually rewarding responses are reinforced by dopamine release in the NAc (Hoebel et al., 1999). Based primarily on animal research, Depue and Collins (1999) found that the NAc, ventral pallidum, and vertical tegmental area dopamine projection system mediates extroversion behavior, which is characterized by positive affect and approach-related activity. Berenbaum et al. (1999) reviewed animal and human studies and concluded that there was converging evidence suggesting that brain dopamine functioning was associated with the experience of pleasure. The *behavioral approach system* (Gray, 1990), responsible for the experience of positive feelings such as elation, happiness and hope, measured by Carver and White (1994) using their behavioral activation system scale (BAS), is primarily modulated by dopaminergic pathways (Stellar & Stellar, 1985). Depue et al. (1994) found that measures of dopaminergic activity were strongly correlated with individual differences on the positive activation (PA) scale measuring approach tendencies devised by Watson, Clark and Tellegen (1988). In his dual control model of male sexual response, Bancroft (1999) describes central nervous system excitatory and inhibitory activity, wherein dopamine plays an excitatory role. Dopamine agonists, according to Bancroft (2002), such as apomorphine, have been used to enhance sexual response, while dopamine antagonists usually results in loss of sexual interest or responsiveness. According to Sachs (2002), dopamine agonists, such as oxytocin and apomorphine, are among the most commonly used and most effective drugs to promote erection, and he notes that animal studies show brain dopamine increases during sexual activity and during exposure of males to sexual stimuli. Berridge (1999) reviews evidence that dopamine is involved in positive emotional states. Zuckerman (1991), discussing theories of monomine functioning, concludes that almost all theories encompass dopaminergic systems in approach, foraging, exploration, sensation seeking, positive affect, attention to the environment, and sensitivity to signals of reward. It is interesting to note that the ascending dopaminergic system tends to be concentrated in the left frontal cortical hemisphere (Tucker & Williamson, 1984), and so left PFC activation could be associated with, or a reflection of, dopamine release (Watson et al., 1999). The prediction is made that in males, dopamine release and activation, especially in the NAc, is positively correlated with different levels of female attractiveness, the more attractive the female, the greater the dopamine release.

There is evidence that the NAc is activated during the experience of pleasant affect (Grant et al., 1996; Hoebel et al., 1999; Koch et al., 1996; Lang et al., 1998; Volkow et al., 1997). In studies using brain imaging techniques, such as MRI and PET, pleasurable memories of cocaine users were associated with activation of the amygdala and nucleus accumbens (Grant et al., 1996; Volkow et al., 1997). "The nucleus accumbens (NAc) is an extension of the amygdala that translates the emotions into action by reinforcing actions that reduce fear and get pleasure" (Hoebel et al., 1999, p.559). Although Lang et al. (1998) points out that, "Neither startle reduction in 'safe' environments nor the inhibition found in the context of reward require amygdala activation" (p. 1254), they note that pleasure-attenuated startle does depend on an intact nucleus accumbens (Koch et al., 1996). Individuals with increased left prefrontal cortex (PFC) glucose metabolism from PET findings, according to Abercrombie et al. (1996), have a decreased metabolic rate in the amygdala, which may be responsible for the dampening of negative affect, the shortening of its time course in individuals who appeared to be more resilient, and may also facilitate the maintenance of approach-related positive affect. Similarly, on the basis of positron emission tomographjy (PET) measurement of regional brain glucose metabolism, Sutton et al. (1997) reported that positive affect was associated with left-sided metabolic increases in the pre- and postcentral giri. Ketter et al. (1996) found that self-reports of euphoria, induced by intravenous procaine, correlated negatively with amygdala blood flow. The predictions are made that there will be a positive correlation between level of female attractiveness and male NAc activation and left PFC glucose metabolism, and a negative correlation between female attractiveness and male amygdala blood flow; the more attractive the female, the higher the male NAc activation and left PFC glucose metabolism, and the lower the amygdala blood flow.

Hoebel et al. (1999) present an intriguing, "...neurochemical, neuroanatomical theory of motivation..." (p. 558) related to appetitive behavior (eating and mating), based primarily on animal research, in which, "...dopamine released from the neurons in the forebrain (nucleus accumbens) helps reinforce successful connections between cognitive inputs and behavior outputs, so the animal learns and repeats the successful behavior" (p. 558), which is basically a "go" or approach disposition. Dopamine, according to Hoebel et al., is released from neurons in the NAc that reinforces connections between input stimuli, such as food or an available sex partner, and responses, such as eating or copulation. NAc translates emotions into action by reinforcing actions that get pleasure and is thus a crucial brain region for go/stop decisions (Hoebel, et al.). Dopomine reinforces various successful innate acts that activate the reinforcement circuits through the hypothalamus (Hoebel et al., 1999; Schizgal, 1999; Wise, 1982). "The mechanisms of reinforcement are as important to economics and psychology as the mechanisms of gravity are to a physicist" (Hoebel et al., p. 562). When a male looks at and has sex with an attractive female, I propose that pleasure inducing dopamine is released by neurons in his NAc, reinforcing the acts of looking at and/or having sex with, this appealing female, and so the male is predisposed to continue and to repeat these pleasurable experiences, a "go" approach orientation (i.e., instantaneous utility).

There is considerable agreement that male sexual interest and desire are associated with gonadal hormones, especially testosterone (Bancroft, 1989, 2002; Regan & Berscheid 1999; Zuckerman, 1991). A decrease in the level of circulating androgens, for example, reliably results in a decrease of sexual desire in males, and an increase in androgen levels produces an increase in sexual desire (Rabkin, Rabkin & Wagner, 1995). Bancroft (2002) makes the point that, "normal levels of testosterone are necessary, but not sufficient for, normal levels of sexual desire" (p. 17). Mazur and Booth (1998) argue that circulating testosterone in males explains little about the variation of sexual behavior as long as the hormones are within the normal range. Testosterone levels in normal young men, according to Zuckerman (1991), however, seem to be related to sexual motivations, sensation seeking (disinhibition), sociability, heterosexual interest, social dominance, and extraversion. Zuckerman (1991) points out that testosterone influences behavior, but that various experiences can increase or decrease testosterone levels, a two-way street. There is also modest evidence for the heritability of gonadal hormone functions (Zuckerman, 1991). In almost all studies to date, testosterone has been associated with sexual *desire* or activity, but not with sexual arousal (Rosen & Beck, 1988; Regan & Berscheid, 1999; Zuckerman, 1991). Sexual desire is purported to be produced primarily by sexual arousal, and so the prediction is made that testosterone levels during male sexual arousal and desire are positively correlated with exposure to different levels of female attractiveness, the more attractive the female, the higher the testosterone level. The testing of this prediction would be facilitated by the simple saliva test of free testosterone (Dabbs, 1991; Dabbs, et al., 1995; Mazur & Booth, 1998).

PROPOSITION 5: PLEASURABLE MALE SEXUAL AROUSAL BY FEMALES IS EXPRESSED THROUGH MALE AUTONOMIC REACTIONS, SOMATIC AND BEHAVIORAL EXPRESSIONS, AND SELF-PERCEPTIONS OF PLEASURABLE SEXUAL AROUSAL THAT REFLECT MALE PREPARATION AND ACTION DISPOSITIONS TO CONTINUE AND TO REPEAT THESE EXPERIENCED PLEASURES.

Activation in males of neurochemical substrate (presented in Proposition 4 above) in response to viewing and/or having sexual relations with a real, live, nude attractive female, is proposed to be instrumental in the production of, or associated with variations in: (a) autonomic heart rate and skin conductance, (Lang et al., 1998); (b) somatic and behavioral reactions of facial expression, *Duchene smile*, timing of smile, bilateral facial symmetry (Ekman, 1992), facial muscle action (Ito & Cacioppo, 1999; Lang et al.), eye blink reflex (Lang, 1995), erection (Bancroft, 1989; Janssen, 1995), picture processing time (Lang et al.); and (c) the awareness of pleasurable sexual arousal evaluated by self-perception measures described in Proposition 11 below in Chapter 3.

Heart rate and skin conductance, according to Lang et al. (1998), are two autonomic functions that are associated with affective experience. Viewing pleasant pictures, such as nude females, prompts greater heart rate acceleration (Lang et al.). Regardless of picture valence (pleasant or unpleasant), "Skin conductance activity co-varies positively with judged arousal, increasing monotonically with increases in rated arousal..." (Lang et al. p. 1252). Lang et al. also note that, regardless of valence, subjects allocate more processing time to arousing, intense images.

Distinctive universal expressions have been found for enjoyment, anger, fear, disgust and sadness by coding videotaped facial expressions (Ekman, 1992). Positive and negative emotions have been associated with distinctive facial actions in neonates, adults and the congenitally blind (Ekman & Friesen, 1982) with the use of the Facial Action Coding System (FAS), developed by Ekman and Friesen (1978). Of particular interest for male sexual arousal is the *Duchenne smile* (Ekman, 1992, 1993), which distinguishes a fake smile from a genuine expression of enjoyment, and involves the involuntary action of the lateral portion of the *obicularis oculi* muscle orbiting the eye (Ekman, 1993). The suggestion is also made by Ekman and Friesen (1982) that enjoyment smiles can be distinguished from other forms of smiling by the timing of the smile and the extent of bilateral symmetry. Ekman (1992) "...posits a central hard-wired connection between the motor cortex and other areas of the brain involved in directing the physiological changes which occur during emotion" (p. 35), such as the *Duchenne smile*. Another approach used to evaluate emotional facial expressions is facial electromyography (EMG) (Ito & Cacioppo, 1999; Tassinary & Cacioppo, 1992). Facial EMG is especially useful in the study of weak emotional processes, as EMG measures muscle action potential rather than the overt effects of the muscle action potentials (Ito & Cacioppo, 1999). In response to moderately pleasant and unpleasant slides of natural scenes, "...EMG activity over the brow (*corrugator supercilli*) and periocular (*orbicularis oculi*) muscle regions varied as a function of the valence and intensity of the subjects' affective reactions to the scenes," (Tassinary & Cacioppo, 1992, p. 29). The more a person liked a scene, the lower the level of EMG activity over the brow region, and the higher the activity in the periocular region and *zygomaticus major* muscle regions (Lang et al., 1998; Tassinary & Cacioppo, 1992). In addition to measuring the valence and intensity of pleasant and unpleasant emotions, FAS and EMG techniques can be useful as indexes of the beginning and end of an emotional episode (Davidson, Ekman, Saron, Senulis & Friesen, 1990).

Lang (1995) reports that the startle blink reflex is increased when a person is experiencing aversive or negative affect, and reduced when experiencing pleasurable positive affect. When viewing pictures rated high on sexual pleasures (e.g., an attractive semi nude couple), the blink reflex was inhibited and small, and as pleasant pictures are judged more arousing, inhibition of the startled reflex increases (Lang, 1995). In an extensive review of the human startled eye blink literature, Filion, Dawson & Schell (1998) conclude that, "The human startle eye-blink reflex is reliably modified by both cognitive and emotional processes" (p. 1). It is interesting to note that the attenuation of the startle reflex during pleasurable experiences depends on an intact nucleus accumbens (Koch et al., 1996), and that, "The findings that the mesolimbic dopamine system is involved in this phenomenon suggests that other parts of the complex limbic-striatal-pallidal circuitry that governs reward-related behavior…might also be relevant for the reduction of the ASR (acoustic startle response) in the presence of a stimulus that predicts reward" (Koch & Schnitzler, 1997, p. 45). Combining the special importance that Hoebel et al. (1999) attached to NAc activity and dopamine release during pleasurable emotional experiences, with the finding that the NAc and dopamine are associated with the reduction of the acoustic startle response in rewarding situations (Koch et al, 1996; Koch & Schnitzler, 1997), suggests a hypothesis derived from the Hoebel et al. (1999) theory that involves the startle-reflex technique (Lang, 1995). Specifically, a male looking at an attractive nude female will have a reduced startle reflex associated with the pleasurable experience produced by the release of dopamine in his NAc.

Male sexual arousal is an innate response to viewing a live, nude female and/or having penile-vaginal intercourse with a female. Erection in normally functioning males, under normal conditions, in response to viewing a nude female is here purported to result primarily from the activation of the neurochemical substrate described above in Proposition 4 (similar to the neurochemical influence on the autonomic, somatic, and behavioral arousal expressions just described). Erection is thus considered to be a relatively automatic response, but more vulnerable to ideation and environmental input (Sachs, 2000) than neurochemical substrate reactions. The proposed automaticity of erection in response to viewing a nude female is consistent with the views of Janssen (1995), and Janssen et al. (2000), as well as the views of Masters and Johnson (1970). "Erections develop just as involuntary and with just as little effort as breathing" (Masters & Johnson, 1970, p. 196). There is considerable agreement that males universally have an innate capacity to respond with sexual arousal to genital stimulation (Allgeier & Wiederman, 1994; Beach, 1956; Byrne, 1986; Freud, 1977; Hardy, 1965; Masters & Johnson, 1966; Reich, 1973; Whalen, 1966), that includes supporting cross-cultural research (Ford & Beach, 1951; Kardener, 1945). These data support the universality of male innate capacity to respond with genital excitement during sexual intercourse with females. Finally, self-report measures of experiencing sexual arousal when viewing females will be described in Proposition 11 below in Chapter 3.

The predictions are made that different levels of female attractiveness will be positively correlated with the male responses of: (a) autonomic functions of heart rate and skin conductance (Lang et al., 1998), (b) somatic and behavioral reactions of FAC activity, especially with intensity of the *Duchenne smile* (i.e., *obicularis oculi* muscle orbiting the eye), as well as timing of the smile, and extent of bilateral symmetry (Ekman, 1992, 1993; Ekman & Friesen, 1978), facial EMG measures of direction and intensity of activity in the periocular and *zygomaticus major* muscle regions (Ito & Cacioppo, 1999; Tassinary Cacioppo, 1992), magnitude of erection (Bancroft, 1989; Janssen, 2000), picture processing time (Lang et al.,), and (c) self-reports of sexual arousal. Negative correlations are expected between level of female attractiveness and male: (b) somatic reactions of EMG activity in the *corrugator supercilli* and *orbicularis oculi* regions (Ekman, 1993), and with amplitude of the eye blink reflex (Lang, 1995).

The proposal is made that the neurochemical substrate, described in Proposition 4 above, of male sexual arousal in response to viewing a live, nude female reflects most clearly and directly selectivity/spontaneity, automaticity, and encapsulation/intractability (Buss, 1984; Ohman & Mineka, 2001), and is totally unconscious (Izard, 1993; LeDoux, 1996; Rosen & Schulkin, 1998; Zajonc, 1998). Autonomic, somatic, behavioral and self-report responses in male sexual arousal to viewing a nude female are proposed to be progressively lower (i.e., self-report lowest) in selectivity/spontaneity, automaticity, encapsulation/intractability, and unconscious to conscious levels, in that they are progressively more influenced by ideation and learning.

PROPOSITION 6: THE SEXUAL JOY EXPERIENCED WHEN A MALE VIEWS AND/OR HAS SEX WITH A LOVELY FEMALE SERVES AS THE CORE REINFORCEMENT OF HIS APPROACH ORIENTATION TOWARDS FEMALES.

The contention of this thesis is that the major and necessary reinforcement of almost all male sexual behavior concerning females, especially sexual desire, are the male arousal delights of viewing, first and foremost, and/or having sex with beautiful females, quintessentially exemplified by orgasmic ecstasy. The capacity and predisposition has evolved in males to experience intense subjective visual pleasure and great physiological tactile enjoyment, especially genital arousal, when viewing and physically connecting with attractive females. This joy reinforces these visual and physical acts and thus incites a desire for continued and additional like enjoyment, and so we procreate. I would define male "libido" as the capacity and predisposition to be pleasurably sexually aroused by the sight of, and physical contact with, an attractive, nude, live female. The experience of sexual delight is thus profoundly significant for male sexuality, and yet there is an extreme dearth of research on interactions with females that enhance male sexual enjoyment, especially pleasurable male sexual arousal to females (Bancroft, 1989; Janssen, 1995; Rosen & Beck, 1988), or on the general enhancement of pleasure (Kahneman, Diener & Schwartz, 1999; Zuckerman, 1987). Kahneman et al. note that, "Another characteristic of past research is the remarkable accentuation of the negative" (p. ix). Zuckerman (1987) comments that, "For some reason most of our theories do not account for positive emotions but focus entirely on the unhappy triad I have called the 'FAD' (fear, anger, and depression)" (p. 221). "The factors that contribute to the diminished experience of pleasure have received surprisingly little attention" (Berenbaum, 1999, p. 275). Janssen (1995) indicates that most studies of sexual arousal are based on clinical emotions such as performance anxiety (Masters & Johnson, 1970), and that almost nothing is known about positive mood states and male sexuality. Ryan and Deci (2001), in their *Annual Review of Psychology* chapter concerning "happiness," never refer to sex anywhere in their paper. Cacioppo and Gardner (1999a), and Cacioppo, Gardner, and Berntson (1999b), describe a ""negativity bias" wherein people tend to respond more strongly to negative stimuli than to positive stimuli of the same intensity. Davidson (2000) indicates that there is less evidence about positive affect, compared to negative affect, in part because positive affect is much more difficult to elicit in the laboratory, and because of the "negativity bias" (Cacioppo & Gardner 1999a), perhaps as a result of evolutionary pressure to avoid harm. Maslow (1954), who studied healthy and creative people, also pointed out the negative emphasis in psychology.

> Maslow upbraided psychology for its "pessimistic, negative and limited conception" of humans. He felt that psychology had dwelled more upon human frailties then upon human strengths; that it had thoroughly explored the sins while neglecting the virtues. Psychology had seen life in terms of an individual making desperate attempts to avoid pain rather than in taking active steps to gain pleasure and happiness. Where is the psychology, Maslow asked, that takes account of the gaiety exuberance, love and well-being to the same extent that it deals with misery, conflict, shame, and hostility? Psychology "has voluntarily restricted itself to only half of its rightful jurisdiction, and that the darker, meaner half." Maslow attempted to supply the other half of the picture, the brighter, better half, and to give a portrait of the whole person (Hall et al., 1998, p. 446).

Could it be that we underestimate the importance of joy in our lives and so study it less, and overestimate the significance of distress in our lives, and so study it more? The framework and direction of sexuality research, I believe, may be influenced by the questions posed for investigation. The question, "What turns me off sexually?" could lead to exploring ways of preventing being turned off, while the question, "What turns me on sexually?" may suggest finding out how to enhance sexual pleasure, as it did for the present writer. A "prevention focus" (Higgins, Grant & Shah, 1999), which involves self-regulation that emphasizes safety-responsibility and an avoidance strategy, would follow from the first question, and a "promotion focus" (Higgins et al.), that includes self-regulation that stresses accomplishments and aspirations and approach as a strategic means, would follow from the second question. Some clinicians, including Freud (1977), had a "prevention focus" according to Higgins (1997), where the production of pleasure and the avoidance of pain was conceptualized in terms of lowering tension. Other psychologist, Higgins (1997) notes, such as Rogers (1961), and I would add Maslow (1954) and Goldstein (1939), had a "promotion focus" where pleasure and pain are derived from achieving or not achieving goals, aspirations, and well-being. The tradition in sexology, and in particular sex therapy, has been predominantly focused on prevention (Regan & Berscheid, 1999), such as the reduction of anxiety in sexual desire disorders (Kaplan, 1979), and the reduction of performance anxiety and spectatoring in the Masters and Johnson (1970) therapeutic approach, although sensate focus certainly has a promotion of pleasure objective. The goal of the present book is to promote and enhance the natural and necessary disposition of males to experience sexual pleasure in response to attractive females, a "promotion focus."

The major exception to the above noted research emphasis on displeasure and pathology, is the introduction of "hedonic psychology" by Kahneman et al. (1999), whose book intends to study enjoyment and well-being. The research goal of hedonic psychology is to maximize human happiness (Kahneman et al.). There is a long history of the hedonic concept that people are motivated to approach pleasure and avoid pain (Fortenbough, 1975; Higgins et al., 1999; Zajonc, 1998). "Aristippus, a Greek philosopher from the fourth century B.C., taught that the goal of life is to experience the maximum amount of pleasure, and that happiness is the totality of one's hedonic moments" (Ryan & Deci, 2001, pp. 143–144). Plato considered pleasure (hêdonê) and pain (lupê) to be the two basic forces of behavior (Fortenbough, 1975). In his *doctrine of hedonism*, Thomas Hobbs states that, "…the underlying causes of all behavior are the tendencies to seek pleasure and avoid pain" (Hilgard, Atkinson & Atkinson, 1979, p. 282).

Jeremy Bentham (1789/1948) wrote, "Nature has placed mankind under the governance of two sovereign masters, *pain* and *pleasure*. It is for them alone to point out what we ought to do, as well as to determine what we shall do…they govern us in all we do, in all we say, in all we think" (p.1). Bentham (1789/1948) attributed behavior to the pleasure principle in his *law of affect*, which stated that people maximize pleasure. He studied hedonics, happiness, joy and the good feelings people have when they engaged in eating, mating, altruism, and profit-taking. He also spoke of pleasure in the release of pain and suffering. Freud (1920/1965) wrote, "It seems that our entire psychical activity is bent upon *procuring pleasure* and *avoiding pain*, that it is automatically regulated by the PLEASURE PRINCIPLE" (p. 365). The hedonic or pleasure principal, according to Higgins (1997), "…has dominated scholar's understanding of people's motivation. It is the basic motivational assumption of theories across all areas of psychology…" (p. 1280). Thorndike (1932) incorporated the hedonic principle in his *law of effect*. "This law states that responses that produce a satisfying effect become more likely to occur again in that particular situation and responses that produce an unsatisfying effect become less likely to occur in that situation" (Hall et al., 1998, p. 510). Higgins refers to Thorndike's law as, "Hedonism of the past…[where] pleasure stamps in…[and]…pain stamps out" (p. 1281). The more precise *empirical law of effect* of Skinner (1953) can also be considered a "pleasure principle" (Higgins). Skinner (1969) was primarily concerned with observable phenomenon, avoided reference to internal events, rejected any reference to satisfying and unsatisfying effects that Thorndike suggested, and referred only to the observable impact a stimulus had on behavior. "Skinner proposed the *empirical law of effect*. That is, a reinforcing stimulus is an event that increases the frequency of behavior with which it is paired, with no reference to 'satisfaction' or any other internal event" (Hall et al., 1998, p. 510). Most of the above conceptions of hedonism (Higgins et al., 1999; Zajonc, 1998) imply a seeking for, or a *desire* for, pleasure, and a seeking to, or a desire to, avoid pain. I propose that the central motivational component of hedonism is first the experience of pleasurable or painful *arousal* that then typically leads to, or produces, a desire to continue and to repeat the pleasurable arousal, and the desire to stop and to avoid repeating the painful arousal. A major proposal of my conceptual framework is that emotional arousal is different from cognitive desire, that arousal typically influences desire, but that arousal and desire are different in structure and function (see Proposition 8). I thus operationally define hedonism as the emotional experience of pleasurable *arousal* that typically leads to the desire to extend and to repeat the enjoyable excitement, and the emotional experience of unpleasant arousal that typically leads to the desire to end and avoid the unsatisfying arousal. (For an alternative view that questions hedonism as a basic motivational source see Ryan and Deci, 2001.) Although hedonistic feelings such as joy or fear, I believe, are usually experienced as conscious cognitions, especially in primary innate perceptual arousals, unconscious pleasurable and painful emotional reactions certainly occur and could influence behavior. Defense mechanisms (A. Freud, 1946), for example, may operate unconsciously to distort reality and so modify pleasurable and painful feelings and their impact on behavior. The hedonic pleasure principle of male enjoyable arousal by appealing females is the central focus of this paper. Mother nature insured procreation by maximizing male sexual delights with females. I believe, in addition, that the innate capacity and predisposition to respond with intense pleasure to the sight and touch of beautiful females is salutary, healthy, required and advantageous. The humanistic psychology of Maslow (1954) and Goldstein (1939), in contrast to behaviorism (e.g., Skinner, 1953) and psychoanalysis (e.g., Freud, 1977), maintains that man has an essential, genetically based, nature of his own, consisting of needs, capacities and tendencies that are good or neutral rather than evil. These organismic theorists stipulate that there is inherently nothing "bad" in the organism; it is made "bad" by a deficient environment. Jean Jacques Rousseau (1762/1979), the French philosopher, proclaimed in his *Emile* that natural man at birth is good, but he can be, and often is, corrupted by his environment which prevents him from acting and developing in accordance with his nature. The very first sentence of Emile is, "Everything is good as it leaves the hands of the author of things, everything degenerates in the hands of man" (Rousseau, 1762/1979, p. 5). The proposal is made that a male's natural, normal, healthy innate capacity and predisposition to experience sexual pleasurable arousal when viewing and/or having sex with attractive females, is a salutary product of evolutionary selection, and the primary reinforcing and motivating force that propels male sexual desire to extend and to repeat these delightful adventures (i.e., an approach orientation).

PROPOSITION 7: THE VISUAL PERCEPTION OF DIFFERENT LEVELS OF REAL, LIVE, NUDE FEMALE ATTRACTIVENESS OBSERVED BY MALES IS THE PRINCIPLE DETERMINANT OF DIFFERENT

LEVELS OF PRIMARY PLEASURABLE MALE SEXUAL AROUSAL BY FEMALES.

A fundamental stipulation of this book is that physiological, behavioral, and subjective pleasurable sexual arousals are directly and primarily dependent on the level of visually perceived attractiveness of real, live, nude females, and the prediction is made that increased levels of observed female beauty will be associated with increased levels of male sexual arousal. Males are the *most* sexually aroused by young, healthy, fertile females ranging in age between 15 and 18. Males are also sexually aroused by attractive females who are 19 years old and older, with progressive and gradual declines in the level of male sexual arousal by females as females get older and thus decline in their resemblance to the Playboy Playmate image. To the best of my knowledge, studies concerned with the comparison between different levels of male sexual arousal and *different levels* of live or even graphic nude female attractiveness, alone or in sex videos, have not been conducted. Most studies of sexual arousal that involve viewing photographs of nude women, or sex videos including nude women (Janssen, 1995; Rosen & Beck, 1988) simply note that males viewed nude females in photos or scenes of sexual activity in a film or video, or gave descriptions of sexual scenes, or were asked to recall such events, or to imagine these activities, but no attention was given to how attractive the females were (i.e., level of female attractiveness), or to how sexually arousing the various graphic or ideational stimuli were *purported to be*. Although Lang (1995) did not differentiate between different levels of "erotica" that were viewed by males as pleasurable and arousing, there was increasing inhibition of the startle reflex as perceived stimuli became more arousing or pleasurable.

Primary pleasurable male sexual arousal is concerned with male sexual arousal to *live*, nude females, and is part of a psychological mechanism based on the adaptations of our ancient male ancestors in their relationships with real, live, nude females. Okami and Schackelford (2001) point out that being aroused by two-dimensional photographs could not represent an adaptation because graphic two-dimensional images of nude women did not exist in the environment of our ancient ancestors. "Being aroused by the sight of live three-dimensional nude young women shows clear evidence of design..." (Okami & Schackelford, 2001, p. 191). Male sexual arousal is the result of an adaptation that was designed by natural selection to serve the function of facilitating reproductive success (Symons, 1979). Arousal to two-dimensional depictions of pornography is a by-product and an estimation of the male adaptation to become excited by the sight of live, young nude women (Okami & Shackelford, 2001). Similarly, Ekman (1992), presuming that emotional facial expressions evolved in situations where actions were perceived through our senses, concluded that, "A symbolic representation of such actions, or a frozen depiction of them in a photograph, should be less likely to call forth an expression, unless the intensity is very high or the person is very prone to a particular emotion" (p. 388).

Male *visual* perception, that plays such a critical and pervasive role in male preoccupation with pornography, promiscuity, and prostitution, has also not been emphasized in the literature (Kinsey et al., 1944; Peterson, 1999; Symons, 1979). "Because a male can potentially impregnated a female at almost no cost to himself in terms of time and energy, selection favored the basic male tendency to become sexually aroused by the sight of females..." (Symons, 1979, p.180). "...the single most uncontroversial example of an adaptation—*is* the eye.... The eye and the rest of the visual system perform no mechanical or chemical service for the body; it is an information-processing adaptation" (Tooby & Cosmides, 1992, p.58). The eye as an information processing adaptation, according to Tooby and Cosmides (1992), constructs cognitive models of the world, including the shapes, locations, orientations of objects, their colors, textures, as well as recognition of faces and their expression. Primary pleasurable male sexual arousal produced by looking at nude females is thus an information-processing adaptation that evolved through natural selection (Algeiers & Wiederman, 1994).

PROPOSITION 8: PRIMARY MALE SEXUAL DESIRE FOR ATTRACTIVE FEMALES IS AN IN THE MOMENT, CONSCIOUS, COGNITIVE APPROACH DISPOSITION RESULTING MAINLY FROM PRIMARY PLEASURABLE MALE SEXUAL AROUSAL BY ATTRACTIVE FEMALES.

The view that sexual *desire* is an innate, biological, motivational force that directs a person to search for sexual objects and activities, has been postulated by several authors (Bancroft, 1989; Bertocci, 1988; Dashiell, 1928; Ellis, 1963; Evans, 1989; Freud, 1977; James, 1890; Kaplan, 1974, 1979; Kraft-Ebbing, 1945; Lichtenberg, 1989; Murray, 1938; Tolman, 1932). According to psychoanalytic theory (Hall et al., 1998), for example, the wish to experience anal, oral, and genital stimulation are inborn instincts that are propelled by the energy of the libido and are aimed at reducing the bodily needs for such stimulation, which results when pleasurable oral anal, and genital excitations occur. The object, in addition, that can satisfy an instinctual oral, anal or genital need is variable, or displaceable in that different objects can satisfy a given need. The desire in the form of an innate instinct appears first, and subsequently anal, oral, and genital arousal reduces the desire or instinct. The above theorists and researchers emphasize an innate biological need arising from within the body that produces, or is expressed as, sexual desire that impels an individual to seek out, or become receptive to, sexual objects and/or experiences (Regan & Berscheid, 1999). These authors, in addition, usually conceptualize the desire for sex and the desire for food as equivalent instincts that enhance survival and reproduction. Some investigators (Beach, 1956; Hardy, 1964; Singer & Toates, 1987) have challenged the above formulations. Beach (1956), for instance, maintains that, "The primacy or innateness of sexual motivation is open to serious dispute...Sexual appetite is...a product of experience, actual or vicarious. The adolescent boys...urges stem more from socio-cultural factors than from those of a strictly physiological nature" (pp. 2,4). All of the above formulations appear to conceptualize "sexual desire" as a *trait* or dispositional attribute that persists over time, in contrast to an in the moment, immediate sexual desire *state* for a certain female at a given moment in time.

In opposition to the above views that sexual desire is primarily an innate trait, or that sexual desire is a trait based mostly on learning, I propose that primary male sexual desire (i.e., a state condition) is produced directly, immediately, at a given moment in time, as a *result* of the innate capacity, predisposition, and emotional arousal experience of males to *respond* automatically with predominantly unconscious, neurochemical, autonomic, somatic and behavioral activation, and with conscious subjective perception of pleasurable sexual arousal (discussed in Propositions 4 and 5 above), when they see and/or have sex with attractive females, that prepares and inclines males to approach these females, which is typically expressed as a desire to continue and to repeat these enjoyable activities. I would maintain that arousal to the taste of delicious food, and arousal to the sight of an attractive nude female, *produces* a desire for that tasty food and for that lovely female. Thinking about past, present or future sexual arousal by, and desire for, females (i.e., cognitive pleasurable sexual arousal and cognitive sexual desire), are considered to be *trait* dispositions that estimate the in the moment, directly, and immediately experienced *state* reactions of primary pleasurable male sexual arousal by females, and primary male sexual desire for these females (i.e., directly viewing and/or having sex with these female). Thinking about past, present, and anticipated sexual arousal and desire are conscious cognitions that are probably influenced more by learning and environmental factors than direct, momentary male sexual arousal and desire, and thus would be less stable and predictable over time.

Webster (1986), in the tradition of not separating male sexuality from female sexuality, defines heterosexuality as, "...the manifestation of sexual desire for a member of the opposite sex" (p. 1063). I maintain, however, that the most critical aspect of male heterosexuality is his sexual *arousal*, when he views and/or physically responds to females, which underpins all of his sexual interactions with females, including his sexual desire. Male heterosexuality, I suggest, should be defined as the innate capacity and predisposition of males to respond with pleasurable sexual *arousal* to the view of, and physical contact with, attractive, live, nude females, which produces a preparation and dispositional desire to continue, and to repeat, these enjoyable experiences and activities.

PROPOSITION 9: DIFFERENT LEVELS OF REAL, LIVE, NUDE FEMALE ATTRACTIVENESS OBSERVED BY MALES ARE THE ESSENTIAL DETERMINANTS OF DIFFERENT LEVELS OF MALE SEXUAL DESIRE FOR FEMALES.

Because male sexual desire is purported to be essentially the outcome of male sexual arousal, which is determined by different levels of female attractiveness, male sexual desire is also dependent primarily on the level of female attractiveness. In contrast to the minimal research conducted on the level of male sexual arousal and the level of female attractiveness, noted above in Proposition 7, a considerable number of studies have been reported on male choice of, and desire for, different levels of female attractiveness, mostly from an evolutionary perspective.

In non-human mammals, the presence or absence of estrus reveals female reproductive value, but in humans who do not advertise ovulation, selection favored male abilities to evaluate reproductive value mostly through visual cues (Symons, 1979). The visual cues that are closely associated with female reproductive value, and hence seen as physically attractive by males, are youth and health, which can be specified in an absolute sense and universally indicates high reproductive value according to Symons (1979). Mostly on the basis of evolutionary perspectives, five female qualities that have been found to be attractive to males, because they were associated with female fertility and health, are: age (Buss, 1989, 1992, 1994; Symons, 1979, 1995; Williams, 1975), curvaceous fat distribution (Singh, 1993a, 1993 b), breast, body, and face symmetry (Singh, 1995; Tovée & Benson, 2000), average height to weight ratio (Tovée, Reinhardt, Emery & Cornelissen, 1998; Tovée & Cornelissen, 2001), and facial neotony (Cunningham, 1986; Cunningham, Roberts, Barbie, Druen & Wu, 1995).

Probably the most important single factor associated with female attractiveness for males, and with female health and fecundity, for our ancient male ancestors and for males today, is female age (Berscheid & Reiss, 1998; Bolig, Stein & McKenry, 1984; Buss, 1989, 1991, 1992, 1994; Buss & Schmidt, 1993; Cameron, Oskamp & Sparks, 1977; Harrison & Saeed, 1977; Jackson, 1992; Jones, 1995; Kenrick & Keefe, 1992; Okami & Shackelford, 2001; Stephan, 1992; Symons, 1979, 1995; Williams, 1975). Buss (1989, 1990), for example, found strong and consistent support for the evolutionary-based hypothesis that males would find the reproductive value of mates, as reflected in youthfulness and physical appearance (i.e., "good looks"), to rank high in importance in 37 different cultures, found in 33 countries, on six continents and 5 islands (N= 9474). Female attractiveness is primarily the reflection of youth and health that signal female reproductive capacity to males in the form of cues such as "…full lips, clear skin, smooth skin, clear eyes, lustrous hair, symmetry, good muscle tone, and the absence of lesions…" (Buss & Schmitt, 1993, p. 208). In all cultures, female reproductive capacity, consisting of reproductive value and fertility, is strongly associated with age (Williams, 1975). *Reproductive value* refers to how many children a woman will have, on average, after a given age (Fisher, 1930), and this value typically peaks in the mid-teens. *Fertility* refers to the age at which reproduction is most likely to occur and it usually peaks in the early to mid 20's (Buss, 1992). According to Buss (1989), men in our evolutionary past who sought short-term mating partners preferred females in their early 20's (i.e., high fertility), while males in our evolutionary past who sought long-term partners would have preferred females in their mid-teens (i.e., high reproductive value). Symons (1995), on the other hand, concluded that in the environment of evolutionary adaptiveness (EEA) selection would have favored males who were sexually attracted most to female cues of reproductive value (i.e., ages 15–18) who desired either short-term or long-term mating partners. Williams (1975) suggests "…a compromise between reproductive value and fertility due to the existence of both long-term mating bonds and some possibility of divorce and extra pair mating" (Buss, 1989, p.2). I agree with Symons (1995) that selection most likely favored males who were most sexually attracted to female cues of reproductive value (i.e., ages 15–18). In his discussion of what men find attractive about women, Stephan (1992) notes that, "From an evolutionary standpoint, the traits that should be considered to be attractive are those associated with fertility—relative youth (optimal age of fertility), health, strength, wide hips, large breasts, and the absence of visible deformities. Thus attractiveness is a surrogate for fertility" (p. 112). Employing an evolutionary model, in contrast to a social psychological model, Kenrick and Keefe (1992), using advertisements from two European countries and from India, and marriage records from 1913 through 1939 on a small Philippine Island, found that as males age they preferred increasingly younger females, whom they found to be more attractive. Young males around 20 preferred females around their own age and as they got older preferred women who were progressively younger than themselves. Kenrick and Keefe (1992) note that, "Maternal age has been associated with increasing health problems for pregnant and nursing mothers, as well as genetic defects in offspring and perinatal mortality (Resnick, 1986)" (p. 78). Other studies which report that males found younger females to be attractive are by Bolig, Stein & McKenny (1984), Cameron, Oskamp & Sparks (1977), and Harrison and Saeed (1977). Age is probably the most important determinant of human female attractiveness according to Williams (1975). Jones (1995), after an extensive review of related literature, concluded that "…there does not seem to be *any* evidence from *any* society that seriously challenges the proposition that physical attractiveness is perceived to decline from younger adults to old age, especially for females" (p. 727).

In a series of significant studies on physical female features related to fertility and reproductive success that males find attractive, Singh (1993a, 1993b, 1994a, 1994b) reported that females with a low waist-to hip ratio (WHR), narrow waist and full hips (WHR around .70), an hourglass figure, were the most attractive to males. In three studies, Singh (1993a, 1993b,) found that in the past 30–60 years, there have been only minor changes in the WHR's of Miss America winners and Playboy centerfolds (i.e., within the range of .68 to .72); that college age men find women with a low WHR to be the most attractive, healthy looking, and to have greater reproductive value; and that males between the ages of 25–85 found women with a low WHR to be more attractive and to have greater reproductive potential. Singh (1993a) reports that a low WHR (i.e., .70) reflected youthfulness, high fertility, and good health (i.e., absence of major diseases, positive endocrine reproductive status, low risk of cardiovascular disease, adult-onset

diabetes, various carcinomas, gallbladder disease and mortality). The above findings were supported by several studies (Barber, 1995; Bjornstorp, 1991; Furnham, Hester& Weir, 1990; Gitter, Lomranz & Saxe, 1982; Gitter, Lomranz,
Saxe & Bar-Tal, 1983; Tovée, Mason, Emery, McClusky & Cohen, 1997; Wass,
Waldenstrom, Rossner & Hellberg, 1997; Zaadstra et al., 1993), including cross-
cultural reports (Furnham, Tan & McManus, 1997; Henss, 1995, 2000; Singh
& Luis, 1995).

From evolutionary perspectives, in addition, fluctuating asymmetry (FA),
body-mass-index (BMI), and facial neotony have been associated with male perceptions of female attractiveness. Singh (1995) found breast asymmetry to be
inversely correlated with attractiveness, and breast symmetry appears to be associated with some aspects of health and fertility (Manning, Scutt, Whitehouse &
Leinster, 1997; Møller, 1995). Breast symmetry had a positive correlation with
fertility in two different samples (Thornhill & Gangestad, 1994). Tovée, Tasker
& Benson (2000) found that males and females found symmetric female images
more attractive than asymmetric images. Alley and Cunningham (1991) suggest
that composite faces are more symmetric, and that is why they are more attractive. Small deviations from bilateral symmetry (i.e., FA) are believed to arise from
an organism's inability to cope with developmental stress, such as from disease,
toxins or parasites (Thornhill & Gangestad, 1995), and if low, with higher fertility (Manning et al.). Livshits and Kobliansky (1991) concluded that, "Individuals
suffering from diverse kinds of morbidity or anomalies of development exhibit a
significant elevated FA in various bilateral morphological structures" (p. 461).
Tovée et al. (1998, 2001), Henss (1995), and Thornhill and Grammar (1999)
argue that the body-mass-index (BMI), measured by dividing height by weight, is
a better predictor of female attractiveness to males than WHR (Singh, 1993a,
1993b), and that BMI is reported to be associated with health and reproductive
potential (Tovée et al., 2001). Tovée et al. (1998, 2001), however, do not indicate the correlation between BMI and age (i.e., youthfulness), which is the key
point, I believe, for predicting fertility, and they do not give the ages of the
women who were rated on attractiveness. They appear to make the assumption
that a woman of 20 with a BMI of 19 (i.e., ideal BMI) would be as attractive to
males as a woman of 50 with a BMI of 19. Employing an evolutionary framework, Jones (1995) reported that males in Brazil, Russia, Ache, Hiwi, and the
U.S. found that attractive females had, "neotenous facial proportions (a combina-
tion of large eyes, small noses and full lips) even after females age is controlled
for" (p. 723). He also found that female models had neotenous cephalofacial proportions in comparison to U.S. undergraduates, and that drawings of faces trans-

formed to make them less or more neotenous were perceived as correspondingly less or more attractive. Jones (1995) believes that because males are attracted to signs of youth (i.e., fecundity) in females, neotenous (i.e., "holding on to youth") facial features are attractive. Shea (1989) and Brace (1995), however, questioned the sexual selection aspects that Jones (1995) attributes to facial neoteny. Cunningham (1986) reported that men found youthful appearance in women to be attractive, and that youthfulness was represented by large eyes, a small nose, prominent cheekbones, and a large smile. Grammar and Thornhill (1994), however, found that small eyes were preferred. Information about levels of ovarian function may be provided by neotenous facial proportions in females, according to Johnston and Franklin (1993).

Almost all of the research reported above on what males find physically attractive in females, and male desire for younger, healthy females, supports the basic premise of male sexual desire presented in this paper. Female beauty for males incorporates the features of youth and health (i.e., fecundity), exemplified by 15 to 18 year old females who have facial and body features that resemble the ideal Miss America or Playboy centerfold females, and these features are most attractive and desirable to males. Because male sexual desire is purported to be determined primarily by male sexual arousal, the above evidence on female attractiveness qualities that men find attractive and desirable (i.e., youth, WHR, BMI, breast body and face FA, and neoteny) also give some support to the contention that male sexual arousal is associated with these female attractiveness features. These assumptions of male arousal, of course, must be directly tested, and research designs for this purpose are presented in proposition 11 below in Chapter 3.

PROPOSITION 10: THE MALE TRAIT OF PLEASURABLE AROUSAL CAPACITY, MALE PERSONALITY TRAITS AND MALE SITUATIONAL APPRAISAL COULD INFLUENCE PLEASURABLE

MALE SEXUAL AROUSAL BY, AND MALE SEXUAL DESIRE FOR, FEMALES.

Primary and cognitive male sexual arousal by, and sexual desire for, attractive females, can of course be influenced by a myriad of factors in addition to the purportedly major cause, level of female beauty. For example, male physical and mental health (Berenbaum, Raghaven, Le, Vernon & Gomez, 1999), age, personality, parental, social and cultural background and development (Kahneman et. al., 1999), and sundry learning experiences; female personality, mannerisms, femininity, affection, prowess as a lover; type of test administered and testing conditions (Rowland, 1999), can all impact on male sexual arousal by, and male sexual desire for, females. These influences, I believe, are the least potent during primary innate pleasurable male sexual arousal (especially unconscious neurochemical, somatic and behavioral activation), and particularly during puberty and adolescence followed by their increased effect on primary male sexual desire, then by their impact on cognitive pleasurable male sexual arousal, and finally effecting the most, cognitive male sexual desire, where the progression is from predominantly unconscious physiological reactivity in primary innate pleasurable male sexual arousal to totally conscious cognitions in cognitive male sexual desire. Three potentially influential areas will be considered as examples in Proposition 10 as they have received attention in the literature (Berenbaum et al., 1999; Eysenck, 1976; Frijida, 1986; Zajonc, 1998; Zuckerman, 1991), namely the trait of arousal capacity (Barenbaum et al., 1999), personality traits (Eysenck, 1965; Zuckerman, 1991) and situational appraisal (Frijida, 1986; Higgins, 1997; Higgins et al., 1999; Lazarus, 1984; Smith & Ellsworth, 1985; Smith & Ellsworth, 1987; Zajonc, 1998).

Male Trait of Pleasurable Arousal Capacity.

There is considerable evidence that there are stable, individual differences in the ability to experience pleasure (Berenbaum et al., 1999), often referred to as hedonic capacity, and there is evidence that hedonic capacity is genetically influenced (Berenbaum et al.). Izard (1993) presents evidence for individual differences in positive and negative emotions that are stable over time in infants and adults that strongly suggest a genetic determination of these individual affective differences. Although male sexual arousal is purported to be due primarily to a male's perception of a female, different males are predicted to experience different levels of sexual arousal *intensity* in response to different levels of female attractiveness, depending upon their different arousal *trait* proclivities (i.e., capacity to experience pleasure). In response to a particular female, for example, one male might assign his highest arousal rating of 10 (in a scale ranging in intensity from 1–10), while the second male might assign his highest arousal score for this same female of 6, where the first male, with a stronger arousal trait disposition, reported scores from 4–10, and the second male, with a weaker arousal trait disposition, indicated responses from 2–6. Both males assign higher arousal scores to more attractive females but the level of their highest scores would indicate different capacities for arousal. The rank-difference-correlation (Guilford, 1950) between the arousal scores of these two males is postulated to be high, as they are both expected to rank or express their arousal scores according to the level of female attractiveness. The prediction is made that the capacity to experience pleasure would influence the level or intensity of male sexual arousal and desire, both primary and cognitive. Males with lower capacity would experience lower levels of arousal and desire intensity, and males with higher capacity would experience higher intensities of arousal and desire. If capacity to experience pleasurable arousal is innate (Berenbaum et al., Izard, 1993), then primary pleasurable male sexual arousal, reflected in innate, unconscious, neurochemical activation, could be impacted first and directly by this capacity to experience arousal, which in turn would influence primary male sexual desire. The intensity of cognitive pleasurable male sexual arousal, and cognitive male sexual desire may also be influenced by arousal capacity. Although undetermined at the present time, it is possible that male capacity to experience pleasure could be normally distributed, with most males being capable of responding with a wide range of sexual arousals, and a small number of males, perhaps 5%-10%, who are capable of responding with either a range of low sexual arousals, or a range of high sexual arousals. In discussing the limbic system and spinal centers complex, as a substrate of sexual behavior, Bancroft (1989) comments that the limbic system and spiral centers complex probably provides the basis of our sexual drive, and that there are considerable individual differences in the arousability of this system that may or may not be normally distributed in the population. He notes that, "…it is reasonable to assume that there will be some individuals who for constitutional or innate reasons, are at the extremes of such a distribution, experiencing either abnormally low or high arousability within this system" (p. 374). I predict, therefore, that *all* males will respond with higher levels of arousal to more attractive females, but for some males, perhaps five to ten percent, the range of arousal intensity will be restricted to low or to high intensities. These individual differences in arousal response intensity disposition could be estimated by the following trait measures. 1. Resting left PFC activation (Tomarkin, Davidson, Wheeler & Kinney, 1992). 2. The self-report Behavioral Approach System (BAS) scale measuring the disposition to react to positive affect stimuli, purported to be responsible for feelings like hope, elation, and happiness (Carver & White, 1994). 3. Positive affect (PA) scale, reflecting one's level of pleasurable engagement with the environment, denoted by such terms as active, interested and enthusiastic (Watson, Clark & Tellegen, 1988; Watson, Wiese, Vaidya & Tellegen, 1999). 4. The self-report Sexual Excitation Scale (SES) measuring sexual excitation tendencies in reaction to sexual stimuli (Janssen, Vorst, Finn & Bancroft, 2002). 5. The propensity to respond with either high or low levels of affective intensity, evaluated by the Affect Intensity Measure (AIM) constructed by Larsen and Diener (1987). 6. Extraversion inclinations evaluating the need for interpersonal excitement, measured by the Eysenck Personality Questionnaire (EPQ) devised by Eysenck and Eysenck (1975). 7. The sensation seeking trait describing the tendency to seek novel and intense stimulation, measured by the Sensation Seeking (SS) scale (Zuckerman, 1994). Although the EPQ and SS scales evaluate a desire for different levels of arousing activities, the assumption is made that this desire reflects a capacity and predisposition to become aroused (Eysenck, 1976, 1997; Zuckerman, 1987, 1991, 1994) that is consistent with the arousal capacity measurements 1–5 above. The prediction is made that there will be a positive correlation between the above seven pleasurable male arousal trait measurements and the perceived level of female attractiveness. The capacity and disposition to be sexually aroused by females may influence the *intensity* of male responses to females. Perhaps the most sensitive and accurate measurement of the disposition to be sexually aroused is resting left PFC activation (Tomarkin et al., 1992), as resting left PFC activity probably represents the most selective/spontaneous, automatic, encapsulated/intractable (Buss, 1984; Öhman & Mineka, 2001) response indicator of the disposition to respond to pleasurable stimulation, in contrast to the other six self-report measures. Individual differences in stable resting baseline patterns of higher left PFC activation were found to be associated with PA (Tomarkin et al. 1992) and with BAS (Sutton & Davidson, 1997) measurements, which appears to support the concurrent and construct validity of left PFC activation as a measure of positive affect disposition and approach orientation. Resting anterior asymmetry in the alpha band demonstrated excellent internal consistency and adequate test-retest (separated by three weeks) stability (Davidson et al., 1992b).

Male Personality Traits.

The level, intensity and variety of male sexual arousals by nude females may be influenced by differences in innate physiological arousal underlying the personality traits of extraversion-introversion (Eysenck, 1967) and sensation seeking (Zuckerman, 1991). Central to Eysenck's (1967) theory of introversion-extraversion and Zuckerman's (1984) theory of sensation seeking are the constructs of optimum levels of stimulation and arousal. "Introverts are said to function and feel better than extroverts at lower levels of stimulation and arousal whereas extroverts function and feel better at higher levels of stimulation and arousal. Thus, introverts and extroverts have different 'optimal levels of stimulation.' The extrovert is said to be characterized by under arousal in non-stimulating conditions and thus must become more active and seek more stimulation to reach a higher level of arousal. The introvert is usually closer to an optimal level [of arousal] even in low-stimulation conditions and therefore does not need to seek stimuli or activity to increase arousal" (Zuckerman, 1991, p. 229). The same optimal levels of stimulation concepts noted above for extroversion-introversion apply to high sensation seeking (i.e., extroversion) and to low sensation seeking (i.e., introversion). One difference is that Esenck's (1967) theory postulates an optimal level of cortical arousal regulated by the reticulocortical activating system, while Zuckerman's (1991) theory proposes an optimal level of catecholamine system activity.

Eysenck (1967) believes that differences in introversion-extraversion result from different levels of activity in the *ascending reticular activating system* (ARAS). ARAS activity stimulates the cerebral cortex, which leads to higher cortical arousal. Introverts, because of their greater ARAS activity, have higher levels of cortical arousal than extroverts, which serve as a causal basis for observed differences on the introversion-extraversion typology. Introverts have lower threshold of ARAS arousal than extroverts. Introverts are predicted to be more aroused, and more arousable, than extroverts. Introverts are distinguished by more excitatory neural processes. Extroverts are distinguished by more inhibitory processes. Differences in emotionality also depend on levels of activity in the limbic system. "Introverts are more sensitive to external stimulation than extroverts, and they are more easily over stimulated than extroverts. Because of the resulting tendency for introverts to avoid excessive stimulation and for extroverts to seek stimulation, Eysenck says that introverts are 'stimulus shy' and extroverts are 'stimulus hungry'. This sensitivity to stimulation is a key characteristic for introverts, because it makes them shy away from any source of intense stimulation. Other people could be one source of intense stimulation, so the introvert tends to avoid people (Hall et. al., p. 378). Hedonic level, or pleasure, is maximized for introverts at low levels of stimulation and for extroverts at high levels of stimulation. There is considerable evidence of a substantial heritable component in individual differences in introversion-extraversion, neuroticism (i.e., emotionality) and psychoticism, and a large body of evidence that supports the biological basis of extraversion and neuroticism (Hall et. al., 1998), although Zuckerman (1991) states that "...a substantial body of research relating cortical arousal levels to *extraversion* has yielded equivocal results..." (p. 272). According to Eysenck's (1967) theory, I would say that males who are introverted may be excessively aroused by a given nude female in contrast to an extrovert who would be only moderately aroused by the same female. Introverts might also be more inclined, perhaps, especially during puberty and adolescence, to be shy and avoid highly arousing nude females than extroverts. Extroverts would seek the stimulation of sexual arousal by enticing females, especially the delights of different and unfamiliar lovely females.

Sensation seeking is "...a trait defined by the seeking of varied, novel, complex, and intense sensations and experiences, and a willingness to take physical, social, legal, and financial risks for the sake of such experience" (Zuckerman, 1994). "...the brain monoamines, dopamine, norepinephrine, and serotonin underlies behavioral mechanisms such as approach, inhibition, and arousal and personality traits like sensation or novelty seeking, impulsivity versus constraint, neuroticism or anxiety" (Zuckerman & Kuhlman, 2000, p. 1019). Serotonin could be considered the brakes and dopamine the accelerator in the drive to risky behavior, with novelty seeking being the core of sensation seeking. Sensation seeking is about positive emotions like joy and the positive feelings produced by novel experiences (Zuckerman & Kuhlman, 2000). Sensation seekers are dedicated to hedonism (Zuckerman, 1991). Zuckerman and Kuhlman (2000) report that the heritability of sensation seeking is around .4, which is toward the high end for personality traits, and about the same as the heritability of extraversion-introversion. According to Zuckerman's (1991) theory of sensation seeking, I would say that the high sensation seekers would be intensely excited by the novelty of new and different lovely nude females, and so more prone to be promiscuous. Low male sensations seekers, on the other hand, maybe more oriented to respond with less intense sexual arousal, and less frequently to a few select attractive nude females, rather than to a wide variety of females.

Male Situational Appraisal.

Situational appraisal theorists (Frijda, 1986; Higgins, 1997; Higgins et al., 1999; Lazarus, 1984; Smith & Ellsworth, 1987), hold that positive and negative affect, including pleasurable male sexual arousal, is produced by, dependent upon, results from a necessary, conscious, situational appraisal. Before a male could respond with joyous rapture to the sight of a live, nude, ravishing female, he would first have to evaluate the situation in terms of his well-being, and this prior cognitive analysis concerning his well-being was a *necessary* prerequisite that actually *produced* his level of sexual excitement (Frijida, 1986; Lazarus, 1984). Frijida (1986) presents a model for the required situational appraisal of one's well-being that produces an emotion, which includes the core components of objectivity, relevance, reality level, difficulty, urgency, seriousness, valence, demand character, clarity, and multiplicity. Another type of situational appraisal is described by Higgins et al. (1999), who believe that positive and negative emotions are generated by recognizing the success or failure of self-regulation or regulatory focus. According to Higgins et al., regulatory focus, "…distinguishes self-regulation with a promotion focus (accomplishments, aspirations) from self-regulation with a prevention focus (safety-responsibility)" (p. 244), the former using approach as a strategic means, and the latter using avoidance as a strategic means. Self-appraisal using a promotion focus leads to cheerfulness when seen as successful and dejection when seen as unsuccessful. Self-appraisal using a prevention focus leads to quiescence when viewed as successful and to agitation when viewed as unsuccessful. Males with a promotion focus may be more inclined to respond with higher sexual arousal by, and sexual desire for, a given female than males with a prevention focus.

I maintain, however, that the emotion of primary sexual arousal (in particular unconscious neurochemical activation) is produced directly and automatically solely by the vision of a lovely nude female. No situational appraisal is a necessary prerequisite to produce the emotion of sexual excitement (see Propositions 3 and 4 above). This cognitive situational appraisal, I maintain, would have negligible impact on primary pleasurable male sexual arousal (i.e., neurochemical activation), and could have, but not necessarily, progressively more and more influence on *conscious* male cognitions involving primary sexual desire, cognitive pleasurable sexual arousal, and cognitive sexual desire male responses. There is only one necessary and essential cause of primary pleasurable male sexual arousal, namely a male's perception of a lovely, nude, live female (Buss, 1984; Davidson, 1992a; LeDoux, 1999; Öhman & Mineka, 2001; Shizgal, 1999; Zajonc, 1980, 1998), and his emotional response and excitement is automatic and based on innate neu-rochemical activation (see Propositions 3 and 4 above). Situational appraisal, I think, could influence the conscious perception of primary pleasurable sexual arousal, primary sexual desire, cognitive pleasurable sexual arousal, and cognitive sexual desire, as these arousal and desire responses reflect or are based on con-scious cognitions that could be effected by conscious thoughts about situational circumstances. In normally functioning males, under typical every day condi-tions, however, I would maintain that primary male sexual arousal, and to a somewhat lesser degree, primary male sexual desire, are influenced predominantly and fundamentally by male visual appreciation of female beauty.

Situational appraisal could, and regularly does, produce emotional reactions, especially in sexually dysfunctional males and females. Situational appraisal, based on development and learning, frequently leads to male anxiety, fear, inhibi-tion, distractions, depression, etc., that are detrimental to sexual functioning, especially primary sexual desire, cognitive sexual arousal and desire, especially cognitive sexual arousal and desire (Bancroft, 1989; Berscheid & Reiss, 1999; Freud, 1917/1959; Kaplan, 1979; Masters & Johnson, 1970; Rosen & Beck, 1988). But the only *necessary* condition that is required to produce fear is a fear relevant stimulus (Öhman & Mineka, 2001), and the only necessary condition that is needed to produce positive or negative affect is an appropriate emotion elicitor (Davidson, 1992a), like a lovely nude female.

3

Measurement and Evaluation of Male Sexual Arousal by Females and Male Sexual Desire for Females.

PROPOSITION 11: RESEARCH METHODOLOGY, INCLUDING THE MEASUREMENT OF PRIMARY PLEASURABLE MALE SEXUAL AROUSAL BY FEMALES AND PRIMARY MALE SEXUAL DESIRE FOR FEMALES, IS REQUIRED TO TEST HYPOTHESES DERIVED FROM EVOLUTIONARY THEORY THAT EMPHASIZE THE CONSTRUCT VALIDITY OF MALE SEXUAL AROUSAL AND DESIRE MEASUREMENTS.

The position of this book is that the most fundamental sexual arousal occurs when a male views a nude, live female. Arousal during copulation includes and requires this visual excitement, and involves more complex physical and psychological interactions during sexual relations between males and females. The same theory and principles applied to visual arousal are applied to genital arousal and orgasm, with the exception that penile-vaginal stimulation and orgasm involve more intense somesthetic excitement. Just as males are innately predisposed to enjoy looking at an attractive female, males are born with the capacity and predisposition to experience intense pleasure during sexual intercourse with an appealing woman. The evidence that males universally are born with the capacity to experience genital pleasure appears incontrovertible (Regan & Berscheid, 1999). Genital arousal is a vital element in evolutionary theory, but for illustrative purposes, the most basic, and more easily measured visual arousal dimension will be evaluated. Ideally real, live, nude females should be observed by males in order to more precisely evaluate primary pleasurable male sexual arousal and primary male sexual desire, but this preferred approach would probably be impractical or perhaps impossible and so photographic images could be used as substitute *estimates* of primary pleasurable male sexual arousal by, and desire for, real, live nude females. Primary pleasurable male sexual arousal by females will be measured by a Male Sexual Arousal by Females Scale (MSAFS). Based on the evolutionary theory that our ancient male ancestors were sexually aroused and attracted by the sight of young, healthy, females (Symons, 1979), MSAFS will include measurements of primary pleasurable male sexual arousal as an emotional response to different levels of female attractiveness.

Male Sexual Arousal to Females Scale (MSAFS)

MSAFS includes a Male Sexual Arousal Scale (MSAS) and a Female Attractiveness Scale (FAS). MSAFS evaluates the basic evolutionary premise that in order to increase reproductive opportunities, males were selected who were most intensely attracted to, and I assume most aroused by, young, healthy, fertile females (Buss, 1994, 1998; Symons, 1979).

1. Male Sexual Arousal Scale (MSAS)

Pleasant sexual arousal is considered to be one type of general pleasurable arousal. MSAS, therefore, consists of measurements that purportedly evaluate pleasurable emotional responses to pleasant stimuli, such as the perception of attractive nude females. Self-report scales that specifically examine sexual excitement are also part of MSAS. The following measurements are included in MSAS. A. *neurochemical substrate*: EEG left prefrontal cortex (PFC) alpha power and recovery time (Davidson et al., 1990; Davidson, 1998a); slow cortical-response (Cuthbert et al., 2000; Lange et al., 1998); dopamine release (Berenbaum et al., 1999; Depue et al., 1994; Hoebel et al., 1999; Wise, 19960); NAc activation (Hoebel et al., 1999); left PFC glucose metabolism (Abercrombie et al., 1996); left amygdala cerebral blood flow (Ketter et al., 1996); and testosterone level (Bancroft, 2002; Zuckerman, 1991); B. *autonomic functions*: heart rate and skin conductance (Lang et al., 1998); C. *somatic and behavioral reactions*: Facial Action Coding System (FAC), including the *Duchene smile*, timing of smile, and extent of bilateral symmetry (Ekman, 1982, 1992, 1993; Ekman & Friesen, 1978); facial electromyography (Ito & Cacioppo, 1999; Tassinary & Cacioppo, 1992); eye blink reflexes (Lang, 1995; Lang et al., 1998); penile erection (Janssen et al., 2000; Rosen & Beck, 1988; Sachs et al., 1999); time spent looking at a nude females (Lang et al., 1998); D. *self-report measures*: Self-Assessment Manikin (Bradly & Lang, 1994; Lang, 1980) and one visual analogue scale (Huskisson, 1974).

The self-report measures in MSAS include the Self-Assessment Manikin (SAM), developed by Lang (1980) specifically to measure the affective valence and intensity of emotional reactions to visual images, including erotic pictures. SAM has excellent psychometric qualities and has been used extensively in emotion research (Bradly & Lang, 1994). A visual analogue scales (VAS1), modified from the VAS constructed by Huskisson (1974), will also be part of MSAS. In VAS1, "no pleasurable sexual arousal" versus "highest imaginable sexual pleasurable arousal" would be placed at either end of a straight horizontal line. SAM and VAS1 can be filled out very quickly by males while viewing a female.

The three components of "instantaneous utility" (Kahneman, 1999; Schizgal, 1999), intensity of sexual arousal, disposition to continue sexual arousal, and disposition to repeat sexual arousal, can be evaluated, for a given male, by the magnitude (i.e., intensity of pleasurable arousal and thus a disposition to repeat arousal), and by the duration (i.e., disposition to continue arousal) of all the above MSAS measures, except for SAM and VAS1, when estimating duration of arousal. Procedurally, a researcher must decide on the practicality and feasibility of using one or more of the above MSAS scales when evaluating male sexual arousal to female attractiveness (FAS). One approach would be to administer different scales, say one or two, on different days. The most important and methodologically sophisticated single arousal test to use in association with female attractiveness is the key measure of PFC asymmetry activation (Davidson, 1992a, 1993), as PFC reaction represents the most spontaneous/selective, automatic, encapsulated/intractable, unconscious biological substrate of emotional response (Buss, 1984; Ohman & Mineka, 2001; Rosen & Schulkin, 1998) to female beauty, and PFC activity is a critical measure of the fundamental approach disposition in male sexual arousal (see Proposition 4). The specific PFC measurements in SAS are: a) the degree of asymmetry between left PFC and right PFC alpha power, the lower the alpha power, the higher the activation, and b) PFC recovery time or time course (Davidson, 1993, 1998a, and see Davidson et al., 1990 for PFC methodology and desiderata issues). Lower left PFC alpha power, and longer PFC recovery time, are predicated to be associated with male perception of higher levels of female attractiveness.

2. Female Attractiveness Scale (FAS)

From an evolutionary perspective, youth and health reflecting fertility are considered to be the primary determinants of female attractiveness for males (Buss, 1994; Symons, 1979). There is robust evidence that as females get older they are perceived by males as less attractive (Buss & Schmitt, 1993; Jones, 1995; Symons, 1979; Williams, 1975). I agree with Symons (1979) that selection favored males who were sexually attracted to female cues of reproductive value (i.e., ages 15–18). The primary criterion of female beauty, therefore, is age, with peak years of female beauty falling between the ages of 15 to 18, with gradual declines in female attractiveness occurring with increasing age. In addition to age, female cues of attractiveness and reproductive value have been found to be associated with female waist-hip-ratio (Singh, 1993a, 1993b, 1994a, 1994b), breast fluctuating asymmetry (Singe, 1995), facial and body fluctuating asymmetry (Alley & Cunningham, 1991; Thornhill & Gangstad, 1995; Tovee et al. 2000), facial neotony (Cunningham et al.1995; Jones, 1995), and body mass index (BMI) (Tovee et al., 1998, 2001). Levels of BMI (i.e., underweight, acceptable, and overweight), however, do not necessarily change with increasing age, and thus does not reflect changes in female attractiveness and fecundity with increasing age. I therefore believe that BMI should be included as a measure of female attractiveness, but BMI cannot be used to test the prediction that increasing female age is associated with decreasing female attractiveness and fecundity. As females get older, therefore, it appears reasonable to assume that WHR, breast and body FA, will increase, and facial neotony will decrease, all suggesting decreases in female attractiveness and fecundity. Eventually of course, the assumptions that with increasing age, WHR, breast and body FA increases, and facial neotony decreases, must be empirically determined by selecting large random female samples between 15 and 60 years of age and testing these predictions cross-culturally. (See Proposition 9 for review of female attractiveness in relation to age, WHR, FA, BMI and facial neotony research.).

FAS ideally should involve real, live, nude females, but for practical research purposes, photo or video depictions of females can be used as *estimates* of male reaction to real, live, nude females. FAS, then, should include graphic depictions of nude females with the following characteristics: (a) age range from 15 to 60, (b) with increasing age, gradual increasing levels of WHR, breast and body FA, and gradual decreasing levels of facial neotony, (c) there should be three levels of BMI (i.e., underweight, acceptable, overweight) for *each age* representing level of WHR, level of breast and body FA, and level of facial neotony,). Varying the levels of WHR, breast and body FA, facial neotony and BMI could be facilitated by using digital manipulation of photographs (Henss, 2000). In the presentation of female graphics, emphasis should be given to simulating, *as close as possible*, real, live, nude females. Perhaps total body life size stationery and video color presentations could be utilized. Various positions, including front, back and side views should be used, as well as the female looking at the camera and her side face profile. Reclining as well as standing positions might be considered. Poses should be included that optimally reflect a curvaceous female body. A time limit, perhaps 1–3 minutes should be set for viewing each pictorial still. A nude female body, I believe, appears more or less beautiful to a male depending on what angle and position the female is in when viewed by a male. Any female angle or position that portrays a less curvaceous, "feminine," youthful look will be seen as less attractive by males. Each female has appealing and less appealing angles and positions. I predict that females between the ages of 16 and 19 will have the greatest number of lovely angles and positions, as judged by males. I propose that the development and standardization of the International Affective Picture System (IAPS: Center for the Study of Emotion and Attention, 1994), devised by Lang, Bradley and Cuthbert (2001), be used as a model in the development and standardization of the FAS. The IAPS consists of color photographs purported to elicit two primary emotion dimensions, one of affective valence, ranging from pleasant to unpleasant, and one of arousal, ranging from calm to excited (Lang et al.,). Because an existing graphic female data base, as suggested above, does not exist to the best of my knowledge, the construction of the proposed FAS scale presents the greatest methodological challenge, and perhaps shortcoming, of the present paper. (See Henss, 2000, on female attractiveness methodology.) Ideally, in keeping with evolutionary principles, real, live, nude females should be selected (Ekman, 1992; Okami & Schackelford, 2001), who differ on age WHR, FA, BMI, and facial neotony. Standardization of such a scale would be impractical, and, at this time, probably impossible. Eventually, however, FAS measurement with real, live, nude females must be conducted to adequately evaluate the extent to which males are sexually aroused by young, healthy females.

Construct Validity of MSAFS

The basic unit of measurement in MSAFS involves the correlation between FAS scores and one or more MSAS scores. One example would be the correlation between FAS and EMG left PFC recovery times (Davidson, 1998a), where a positive correlation would indicate that with increasing levels of female attractiveness, males responded with longer left PFC recovery time. Each time MSAFS is administered, the association between PFC recovery time and level of female attractiveness evaluates the hypothesis, based on evolutionary theory, that males are sexually aroused by young, healthy females. If correlations between PFC recovery time and female attractiveness are signifiant, therefore, the construct validity (Cronbach & Meehl, 1955) of MSAFS is supported. The specific predictions about male sexual arousal that could support, if significant, or not support, if not significant, the construct validity of MSAFS are that there will be significant positive correlations between FAS and: A. *neurochemical substrate*: left PFC recovery time (Davidson, 1998a); slow-cortical response (Cuthbert et al., 2000; Lang et al., 1998); dopamine release (Berenbaum et al., 1999; Depue et al., 1994; Hoebel et al., 1999; Wise, 1996); NAc activation (Hoebel et al., 1999); left PFC glucose metabolism (Abercrombie et al., 1996); left amygdala cerebral blood flow (Ketter et al., 1996) and testosterone level (Bancroft, 2002; Zuckerman, 1991), B. *autonomic functions*: heart rate and skin conductance (Lang et al.), C. *somatic and behavioral reactions*: FAC, *Duchene smile*, timing of smile, extent of bilateral symmetry (Ekman, 1992; Ekman & Friesen, 1978); facial EMG (Ito & Cacioppo, 1999; Tassinary & Cacioppo, 1992); penile erection (Janssen et al., 2000; Rosen & Beck, 1988; Sachs et al., 1999); time spent looking at nude female (Lang et al.), D. *self-report measures*: SAM (Bradly & Lang, 1994; Lang, 1980); VAS (Huskisson, 1974); two VAS scales to measure sexual desire for females described below under Measurement and Validity of Male Sexual Desire Scales. There will be significant negative correlations between the FAS and: A. *neurochemical substrate*: EEG PFC alpha power (Davidson, 1998b; Davidson et al., 1990), B. *somatic reactions*: eye blink reflex (Lang, 1995). Significant correlations between the FAS and one or more of the above arousal measures, and the self-report desire scales (i.e., VAS2, 3, and 4 described below), would support construct validity of MSAFS.

The seven pleasurable arousal trait disposition scores (i.e., resting left PFC activation, BAS, NA, SES, AIM, E, and SS) noted above in Proposition 10 (under Trait of Pleasurable Arousal Capacity), purported to influence state MSAFS scores, are also assumed to measure stable dispositions of approach behavior, are genetically influenced, and have specific neurochemical substrate (Carver & White, 1994; Davidson et al., 1990; Eysenck & Eysenck, 1975; Janssen et al., 2002; Larsen & Diener, 1987; Watson et al., 1999; Zuckerman, 1994). Pleasurable male sexual arousal, as measured by MSAFS, also postulates that increasing MSAFS scores indicate increasing approach tendencies, and that male sexual arousal has distinct neurochemical substrate, as described in Proposition 4, and is produced by innate capacity and predispositions. Thus, significant correlations between MSAFS scores and the above 7 arousal trait scores would support the construct validity of MSAFS in respect to approach orientation and genetic influences; and where the seven trait score measures report neurochemical substrate that are also noted for male sexual arousal, such as PFC activity and dopamine release (i.e., left PFC activation, BAS, PA, SES and SS), the construct validity of MSAFS, in respect to neurochemical substrate, is supported.

The prediction is also made that MSAFS will correlate negatively with the GRISS measure of sexual dysfunction (Rust & Golombok, 1986), and that low MSAFS scores would be associated with sexual arousal and desire problems, such as erectile and low sexual desire dysfunctions. Significant correlations would support the construct validity of MSAFS, as these predictions are based on evolutionary theory. If our ancient male ancestors were not sexually aroused by young, healthy nude females, they could have certainly suffered from sexual arousal and desire problems, thus reducing reproductive opportunities. The prediction is made, in addition, that MSAFS would be positively correlated with general arousal measures such as the Hulbert Index of Sexual Excitability (Hulbert, Apt & Rabehl, 1993), and the erotophilia-arousal tendency measured by the Sexual Opinion Survey (Fisher, Byrne, White & Kelley, 1988), which would support the predictive validity of MSAFS. Internal and test-retest reliabilities, of course, should also be estimated for MSAFS.

Measurement and Validity of Male Sexual Desire Scales

Male sexual desire could be measured by three visual analogue scales (Scot & Huskisson, 1976; Price, McGrath, Rabie & Buckingham, 1983), evaluating the desire to continue looking at the female (VAS2), the desire to see the viewed female again (VAS3), and the desire to have sexual intercourse with this viewed female (VAS4). In VAS2, "no desire to continue looking at female" could be paired with "greatest desire to continue looking at female." VAS3 might be anchored with "no desire to see again" and "greatest desire to see again." VAS4 might be anchored with "no desire to have sexual intercourse with" and "greatest desire to have sexual intercourse with." These three VAS measures would be filled out at the same time that the MSAS self-report SAM (Lang, 1980) and VAS1 scales are filled out, *during* the viewing of a female.

Significant correlations between VAS2, VAS3 and VAS4 sexual desire scales and the female attractiveness scale (FAS) would support the construct validity of the VAS desire scales, as evolutionary theory (see Proposition 1) holds that male desire (proposed to result primarily from male sexual arousal) to see and have sex with attractive, nude females will increase in strength as female levels of attractiveness increase. Significant correlations between the three VAS desire measures and any of the above MSAFS arousal measurements would support the construct validity of these desire scales, as evolutionary theory postulates that male sexual desire for attractive females is primarily the result of male sexual arousal by these females. The prediction is also made that VAS2, VAS3 and VAS4 will correlate significantly with a general measure of sexual desire, such as the Hulbert Index of Sexual Desire (Apt & Hulbert, 1992), which would support the predictive validity of VAS2, VAS3 and VAS4. Internal and test-retest reliabilities should also be estimated for the VAS2, VAS3, and VAS4 scales.

In all predictions of male sexual arousal by, and sexual desire for, females involving conscious cognitions, the variables of arousal capacity, personality traits (i.e., EI and SS) and situational appraisal (see proposition 10 in chapter 2) must be evaluated as to their possible influences on male sexual arousal and desire. The conscious awareness of sexual arousal by and the conscious desire for, females may be influenced by arousal capacity, personality traits and situational appraisal. In primary perceptual arousal, the unconscious neurochemical, autonomic, somatic and behavioral responses of males when viewing nude females is not influenced by situational appraisal, but may be influenced by arousal capacity and personality.

The methodology presented above to evaluate the fundamental hypothesis, based on evolutionary theory, that males are more highly sexually aroused by more attractive females includes the following unique, or infrequently employed, features. The Male Sexual Arousal to Females Scale (MSFAS) evaluates an actual *interaction* between a specific male and a specific female. The MSFAS measures one male's arousal to one female at a time, representing a certain level of female beauty, at a certain moment in time (i.e., a state reaction), and not to females in general at anytime (i.e., a trait reaction). Male arousal is determined mostly by unconscious, and thus more precise or more valid and reliable neurochemical, autonomic, somatic and behavioral reactions (see Propositions 4 and 5 in Chapter 3), and secondarily by conscious self-perceptions. The Female Attractiveness Scale (FAS) delineates different levels of female attractiveness. Male arousal is evaluated with multiple measurements (neurochemical, autonomic, somatic, behavioral, and self-reports). Each time the MSAFS is administered, evidence to support or to refute the basic hypothesis, based on evolutionary theory, of male arousal being positively correlated with female beauty is supported or not supported (i.e., construct validity evaluation). The momentary immediate reaction of a male to a specific female is an actual example of his real, typical, daily behavior under consideration, and not a male's ideas about how he will act in another, outside the testing situation, real-life experience or condition. Most behavioral tests (Hall et al., 1998) make the assumption that, based on test results, you could predict outside, actual, real-life behavior (i.e., predictive validity), but support for predictive validity is rarely presented. Scores on the Sexual Excitation Scale (Janssen et al., 2002), for example, which purports to measure the propensity for sexual excitation in men assumes, but does not demonstrate, that scores on this test will accurately predict the propensity for sexual excitation of males in their actual, real world experience (i.e., predictive validity). The study of primary pleasurable male sexual arousal by females, as proposed in this book, is extraordinarily difficult. In fact, this type of research is so challenging, it has rarely, if ever, been attempted, or even suggested. If sexology is to advance, however, I believe we must confront significant, meaningful, daily sexual experiences, that have been taken for granted, and thus overlooked. The scientific method notwithstanding, and eventually *always* necessary, we must take the initial plunge into the murky waters of introspection, common sense, multiple causation outcomes, everyday life, the *real world*.

4

Conceptual Framework of Primary Male Sexual Arousal and Desire, Basic Assumptions, Major Principles, Puberty and Adolescence.

My own sexual life history has had a direct and profound influence on the development of my theoretical approach, where personal introspections, for example, were the major source of my primary focus on sexual visual *arousal* by females, that forms the most central and critical theoretical dynamic of my model, and arose from my recognition that in my sexual development my arousal by lovely nude females was the foundation that orchestrated all vital aspects of my sex life. This book, and especially the present chapter, is the result of my endeavors to understand in depth my personal journey of sexual arousal by gorgeous females. Perhaps the most important single reason for my quest to understand the origin, structure, process and consequences of male sexual arousal by females was the central role my own visual (i.e., view of beautiful nude females), and kinesthetic (i.e., orgasmic ecstasies associated with the view and contact with lovely nude females) excitements played in my unfolding sexual odyssey that I experienced with great intensity at puberty and afterwards. My personal insights appear to have been derived in a similar manner by Erikson (1950). "Erikson believed that his own life history had a distinct bearing upon the development of his theoretical outlook" (Hall et al., 1998, p. 90).

FIGURE II. CONCEPTUAL FRAMEWORK OF PRIMARY INNATE MALE SEXUAL PERCEPTUAL EMOTIONAL HEDONIC AROUSAL BY FEMALES AND MALE SEXUAL DESIRE FOR FEMALES.

Evolutionary male psychological mechanism that facilitates reproductive success via gene transmission. Genetic, universal and nomothetic. Propositions 1 and 2.*

Appropriate emotion elicitors: A male looking at a nude female and/or a male sexually interacting with a nude female. Occurs from puberty through adulthood. A state, in the moment perception. Proposition 4.

Arousal capacity and unconscious neurochemical activity underlying the personality traits of extroversion-introversion and sensation seeking (Proposition 10).

Unconscious neurochemical, autonomic, somatic and behavioral responses. Propositions 4 and 5.

Action dispositions: Preparation for approach or avoidance actions. Proposition 3.

Situational appraisal. Proposition 10.

Conscious and/or unconscious motivation by hedonic feelings (e.g., joy or disgust). Proposition 6.

Conscious and/or unconscious desire to continue or stop, to approach or avoid persons, situations, or ideas. Propositions 8 and 9.

---

* Propositions 1–10 can be found in Chapter 2.

BASIC ASSUMPTIONS.

Based on an adaptation to facilitate reproductive success that evolved through natural selection, males possess a psychological mechanism consisting of an innate capacity and predisposition to immediately, automatically, and consistently respond with the emotion of primary pleasurable sexual arousal, that is produced by unconscious neurochemical activation, accompanied by autonomic, somatic, and behavioral responses, that may be influenced by arousal capacity and personality traits (i.e., extroversion-introversion and sensation seeking), and reflected by conscious self-perceptions of this arousal, that may be influenced by situational appraisal, at the moment they look at, and/or have sex with, attractive (i.e., young, healthy, fertile), live, nude females, emerging with intensity around puberty and continuing throughout life; the more attractive the female, the higher the sexual arousal, which reinforces the activities of viewing and/or having sex with these females, that prompts the male to desire to continue and to repeat these delightful sexual experiences, which are good and beneficial for all males and females, past, present and future, as these male sexual delights are the major, only and necessary facilitators of gene transmission.

MAJOR PRINCIPLES.

The following is a description and analysis that summarizes the major principles derived from the above basic assumptions. These major principles comprise a "single domain theory" (Hall et al., 1998, p. 17).

   1. Primary innate perceptual pleasurable male visual and kinesthetic sexual arousal by attractive females is an innate current psychological mechanism that evolved through natural selection as a critical adaptation to facilitate reproductive success.

   a) Primary perceptual pleasurable male sexual arousal by females is the most influential (e.g., in producing sexual desire for females), and the only psychological mechanism that is a necessary, and probably the most powerful, male adaptation enhancing gene transmission, with intensely exciting reinforcement of seeing and having sex with beautiful females.

   b) There is an emphasis on the selection of the highest levels of visual and kinesthetic (especially orgasmic) arousal in order to guarantee reproductive success. Visual and kinesthetic arousal by females may be among the most enjoyable perceptual male experiences, thus insuring incomparable desire for seeing and having sex with females.

c) Male sexual arousal is a response to a specific, restricted, single external stimulus, the female body, perhaps the most precisely delineated external object males are innately programmed to respond to. The taste of many types of sweet and salty foods are innately enjoyed, but only the specific configuration of an attractive nude female body produces pleasurable male sexual arousal. In order to insure reproductive success, the female vision producing excitement had to be unmistakably and clearly prescribed for a male's visual information processing adaptation.

A, b, and c above represent qualities that are *unique* to males and which distinguishes male sexuality, and sexology as a discipline, from all other types of behavior and thus from all other disciplines. These unique male features clearly differentiate male sexuality from female sexuality.

2. Primary innate perceptual pleasurable male sexual arousal by females is a reaction consisting of unconscious *neurochemical*, autonomic, somatic and behavioral activation, which lead to the conscious perception of pleasurable feelings that occur with the release of dopamine (Higgins et al., 1999). The unconscious neurochemical male arousal *reaction* to females is the most critical core foundation that orchestrates male sexuality (e.g., male sexual desire for females). Mother nature could not entrust the vital mission of gene transmission to thinking or cognitions, but she could rely on automatic, unconscious neurochemical activity. It would be disastrous for survival if we had to think before we took a breath or pump blood through our arteries and veins. Neurochemical activation, especially PFC activity (Davidson, 1993) may produce, or co-exist with, autonomic, somatic and behavioral responses. The pleasurable emotional impact on males looking at lovely females can be evaluated by these neurochemical, autonomic, somatic, behavioral and self-descriptions (see Chapter 2, propositions 4 and 5). Until recently, little attention was devoted to neurochemical substrates (Bancroft, 1999; Davidson, 2000a; Hoebel et al., 1999; Lang et al., 1998; Stoléru et al., 1999), autonomic responses (Lang et al., 1998), and somatic and behavioral expressions (Ekman, 1992; Ito & Cacioppo, 1999; Lang, 1995), that may underlie sexual arousal, which are emphasized in the present paper. Eysenck (1997) maintained that *proximal* antecedents (i.e., biological intermediaries) and proximal consequences based on experimental studies conferring causation are, "...the most important aspects of any theory of personality; if verified, they constitute solid evidence for the theory concerned..." (p.1226). The neurochemical substrates of PFC activity, dopamine release, autonomic heart rate and skin conduc-

tance reactions, and the various somatic and behavioral expressions such as eye blink reflex, FAC, *Duchene smile*, facial EMG, are examples of proximal mechanisms that lend themselves to experimentation and inferences about causality.

3. Male sexual arousals by females are "emotional reactions, action dispositions, motivationally tuned states of readiness" (Lang, 1995, pp. 372–374). Emotions reflect central activation and preparation for action. When pleasurable emotions are experienced (i.e., males view and contact with lovely nude females), the prototypical motive system is expressed by behavioral approach. When unpleasant emotions are manifest, the prototypical motive systems is expressed by behavioral escape and avoidance. (See proposition 3 in chapter 2.)

4. Arousal capacity, personality and situational appraisal, (see Proposition 10 in Chapter 2) can influence male sexual arousal by, and male sexual desire for, females. Arousal capacity and the unconscious neurochemical activity underlying the personality traits of extraversion-introversion (Eysenck, 1967) and sensation seeking (Zuckerman, 1994) may modify unconscious emotional neurochemical, autonomic, somatic and behavioral reactions. Situational appraisal could influence arousal awareness and desire. (See Proposition 10 in Chapter 2.)

5. The emotional response of primary pleasurable male sexual *arousal* by females is the "libido," reinforcement, energy source, unparalleled physical rapture, and the most crucial and necessary foundation of male sexuality. Male sexual behavior, especially male sexual desire, is fueled, directed, and enhanced by this emotional reaction that serves the evolutionary goal of reproductive success. The basic emotions of pleasure and pain (e.g., fear, anxiety, depression) produce, by their positive or negative reinforcement, fundamental approach and avoidance orientations.

6. Innate visual, gustatory, olfactory, kinesthetic, and auditory sensory enjoyment that produces an approach orientation, and sensory pain that leads to an avoidance orientation, which facilitates survival (i.e., all five senses), and that enhances reproductive success (i.e., vision of and kinesthetic contact with, a female), are all *inherently good* and beneficial for mankind. Hedonism in the service of evolution is normal, natural, healthy and desirable, with the proviso, of course, and always, that *male satisfaction of hedonistic pursuits and avoidance of pain do not bring any type of harm or discomfort to anyone.* The innate goodness of male sexual arousal highlights the importance of understanding *normal* male behavior in order to enhance this wonderful excitement.

7. Male *visual* perception of a lovely, nude, live female is the most critical, influential and necessary process that produces pleasurable male sexual excitement. The vision of a female is the original, basic, most powerful, important, and

consistent aphrodisiac known to males. All sensory perceptions (i.e., visual, gustatory, auditory, kinesthetic, and olfactory), other than a male's vision of a female, facilitate survival and thus permit reproduction. Only male visual arousal to females, however, directly facilitates and enhances reproductive success and does not facilitate survival per se. The evolutionary goal of enjoying the taste of fresh, sweet fruit is for survival. The evolutionary purpose of male pleasurable visual arousal by females is to facilitate gene transmission. The only perception that facilitates survival or reproductive success wherein deprivation (e.g., no food, insensitivity to pain, etc.) does not cause death is male visual arousal by females. Male visual arousal to females is also the basis of pornography, promiscuity and prostitution. Although male visual arousal to females is stressed, evaluated, and fundamental to all male sexual behavior, kinesthetic arousal from genital stimulation (i.e., intercourse, fellatio and touching) is of course intensely exciting, especially orgasm, and a powerful determinant, in addition to male visual arousal, of male sexual desire for females.

8. Primary pleasurable male sexual *arousal* by females is fundamentally different than primary male sexual *desire* for females.

a) Primary pleasurable male sexual arousal by females is an emotional reaction to an external stimulus (i.e., female body) based on predominantly unconscious neurochemical activation (i.e., PFC activation and dopamine activity, see Proposition 4 in Chapter 2). Primary male sexual desire for females is an internal, conscious cognitive attitude directed outward toward females and is based on neuroanatomical structures similar to all conscious attitudes and cognitions (Davidson, 1984).

b) Primary pleasurable male sexual arousal, in contrast to male sexual desire, includes autonomic, somatic and behavioral expressions, in addition to, and perhaps caused by, neurochemical activation.

c) Primary pleasurable male sexual arousal by females, especially unconscious neurochemical activation, is more stable and predictable than primary male sexual desire. Primary pleasurable male sexual arousal is an innate capacity and predisposition to respond automatically with pleasurable affect to attractive females. Although the level of primary male sexual desire is produced primarily by the level of primary pleasurable male sexual arousal, primary male desire is a cognition that could be influenced more by other cognitions and sundry environmental factors. On any given occasion, and under normal conditions, I would speculate that primary sexual desire would be fairly stable and consistent with primary pleasurable sexual arousal, but primary pleasurable sexual arousal would be extremely predictable as a reaction to females, certainly as far as neurochemical activation is concerned. The conscious self-perception by males of their sexual arousal by females is certainly vulnerable to cognitions influenced by learning and environmental factors, but conscious arousal is typically private, and not open to nearly as much scrutiny as desire.

d) Primary pleasurable male sexual arousal is the central figure and orchestrator of gene transmission, and so mother nature insured stability by neurochemical activation in males to the sight of, and contact with, females. Primary pleasurable male sexual arousal by females in terms of neurochemical reactivity is equivalent in stability and consistency overtime to enjoying the taste of delicious sweet food, like sweet fresh fruit, the former an adaptation necessary for reproductive success, the later an adaptation necessary for survival. Primary male sexual desire must be part of the evolutionary scheme, of course, for reproductive success, but a cognitive wish cannot be as stable as unconscious physiological reactivity.

e) Primary pleasurable male sexual arousal is almost always enjoyable, and could be very intense, as in orgasm. Primary male sexual desire can be strong, and if female rejection is involved, painful.

Cognitive pleasurable male sexual arousal and cognitive male sexual desire, where males think about, but are not looking at live or graphic representations of females, are both conscious cognitions and so subject to learning and environmental influences that could lead to unknown degrees of stability/instability for different males on different occasions, over different periods of time. Most past research concerning male sexual arousal has dealt with low levels of arousal, typically using penile tumescence as the measurement of arousal (Jansen, 2002; Rosen & Beck, 1988). Research dealing with male sexual desire has been predominantly on cognitive sexual desire where male opinions about their sexual desire are noted on paper and pencil tests (Buss, 1994; Regan & Berscheid, 1999).

9. Primary pleasurable male sexual arousal by females involves "*capturing the moment,*" a *state* reaction, instantaneous utility (Shizgal, 1999), in vivo observation, real-life experiences, especially the rapture of being sexually alive. I want to capture the moment when a male gazes at a blazingly gorgeous, live, naked female and is blown away by her rapturously bewitching and seductive pulchritude. The heart of my model is this instantaneous, automatic, momentary, joyous sexual arousal emotion that occurs when a male looks at a lovely real, live, nude female, which in turn produces a sexual predisposition to approach and relate to this enticing woman. Evolutionary theory predicts that males are excited by the view of real, live, attractive females (Okami & Shakelord, 2001). In contrast to

my focus on real, momentary male sexual arousal by females (i.e., state responses), most of the research in sexology has dealt with sexual arousal and sexual desire as characteristics that a person exhibits overtime, predispositions measured by questionnaires purported to predict actual, real life behavior (i.e., a personality response trait). All theories of personality (Hall et al., 1998) also represent traits such as introversion-extroversion (Eysenck & Eysenck, 1975), self-actualization (Goldstein, 1939), sensation-seeking (Zuckerman, 1994). My focus is on primary pleasurable male sexual arousal by, and primary male sexual desire for, females (see Chapter 1 Overview), which emphasizes, and directly measures, in the moment, immediate male reactions to a specific, ideally live female. My unit of measurement, if possible, is a male's reaction to a specific live female that is complete at the time of observation or testing and is not only an assumption about this males behavior at some other time. Each time I demonstrate congruence between the level of the male's sexual arousal to the level of beauty of a specific female at a certain moment in time, I am supporting my evolutionary based theory (i.e., construct validity). In contrast to my approach, almost all other theoretical or observational orientations that I am aware of deal with cognitive pleasurable male sexual arousal and cognitive male sexual desire (see Chapter 1 Overview), representing trait dispositions, where males think about females, and where the assumption is made that responses to live females in the real world outside the laboratory is accurately predicted by questionnaire responses about females in general (i.e., predictive validity), an assumption that is actually rarely evaluated or supported. Where graphic representations of females are used to evaluate primary pleasurable male sexual arousal, usually involving low levels of arousal measured by penile tumescence or questionnaires (Rosen & Beck, 1988), again the assumption is made that penile tumescence or questionnaire responses can be generalized to real life situations, and to women in general, an assumption that is rarely tested. I am calling for sexology research to return to the real world, to our actual, significant and meaningful daily experiences.

10. The level of primary pleasurable male sexual arousal by females is proportionate to female beauty, the greater the female beauty the higher the male arousal. The *level of female beauty*, from unattractive to very attractive, is of cardinal importance in my theoretical model as a crucial determinant of different levels of male sexual arousal. All previous research to date on male sexual arousal by, and male sexual desire for, females (Buss, 1989, 1994; Regan & Berscheid, 1999; Rosen & Beck, 1988) has not made this vital calibration of degree of female beauty. Even though I have presented guidelines for such a measurement in Chapter 3, Proposition 11 (i.e., FAS), based on the presented theoretical model,

the formulation, or rather the lack of formulation, for such an instrument is perhaps the most serious limitation of my research design. In addition, ideally the FAS should involve real, live nude females in order to more accurately determine if the level of male sexual arousal is positively correlated with the level of female beauty. The availability and calibration of live females, even for age alone (i.e., selecting highest or average beauty for a given age), is quite formidable, but must eventually be accomplished. (Are there any male graduate students out there who are willing to take on this daunting, challenging, wildly exciting task?) A scale of female beauty, I suggest, is predominantly dependent upon female age and is thus a developmental scale first and foremost. The qualities of health and fertility associated with different ages, such as WHR (Singh, 1993a, 1993b) are also incorporated (see Chapter 3).

11. Primary pleasurable male sexual arousal by attractive females involves automatic male arousal to *all* attractive females, and so males are inclined to seek and enjoy a *variety* of sexual encounters. After an extensive review of popular and professional literature and cross-cultural investigations, Symons (1979) concluded that, "Presently available evidence supports the view that human males typically experience an autonomous desire for variety of sex partners..." (p. 250). Males are so constituted that they resist widespread and powerful forces, such as the church, government, legal and police authorities, and the glorification of monogamy, that operate to prevent or curtail a male's desire for variety (Peterson, 1999; & Symons, 1979). "There seems to be no question but that the human male would be promiscuous in his choice of sexual partners throughout the whole of his life if there were no social restrictions. This is a history of his anthropoid ancestors, and this is the history of unrestrained human males everywhere" (Kinsey et al., 1948, p. 589). Eysenck and Wilson (1979) note that the male tendency is to be polygamous and that the "...male interest is to impregnated as many eggs as possible" (page 82), so men are constantly searching for attractive females. "The primary benefit of casual sex to ancestral man was a direct increase in the number of offspring, so that men faced the key adaptive problem of gaining sexual access to a variety of different women" (Buss, 1994, p. 76). The male interest in female variety noted by the above authors, I propose, is fundamentally due to their innate capacity and predisposition to be sexually aroused by *all* attractive females that they see and have sex with, which, in turn, produces their prodigious sexual appetite.

PUBERTY AND ADOLESCENCE.

Perhaps the most critical and influential period in the sexual development of heterosexual males occurs during puberty and adolescence because of the emergence of powerful, evolutionary based, innate, automatic, intensely exciting arousal to attractive females, especially lovely, real nude female. Innate male perceptual and sexual arousal by females is the *only* innate perceptual arousal of all five sense modalities that is exclusively devoted to facilitating reproductive success, and the only innate perceptual arousal that is first manifest with intensity and clarity around puberty after several years of conditioning and learning, and within a complex social environment which includes a multitude of forces (e.g., females, parents, church, media) that may impede, frustrate, instill guilt, or on the other hand, support, encourage and reduce guilt, in males. Innate perceptual arousal to the taste of sweet fresh fruit, for example, is an evolutionary design devoted to survival, not reproductive success, which appears to be present at birth, and is supported and value throughout life. Pre-pubertal male sexual experiences such as curiosity about the female genitals, or pleasurable penile stimulation certainly occurs, but they are not innate, compelling or driven by evolutionary demands, and thus infrequently become focal points of major interest and excitement until around puberty when the attractive naked female body becomes an obsession and the source of extreme pleasure and/or frustration. All innate perceptual emotional arousals, with the exception of innate sexual arousal, including the taste of sweet food, body comfort, pleasant sounds, sight and orders, which are required for survival are typically supported and accepted as good and necessary by society. Innate male sexual arousal by females, an equally potent and necessary evolutionary force insuring gene transmission, emerges at puberty into a complex social structure after years of conditioning and learning that presents mixed messages, conflicting opinions and certainly rarely clear-cut support and encouragement for this intensely experienced and powerful disposition. I propose that the enormous force and pervasive impact of a male's innate sexual arousal to beautiful female bodies around puberty sets into motion the formation of a basic foundation for sexual behavior and development. Pre-pubertal perceptual and learning experiences of course will influence what occurs during puberty and afterwards, but I suspect that the most important impact that will form the fundamental foundation of sexual behavior and development for males are the sexual experiences that take place during puberty and adolescence, within an influential social-cultural environment, when powerful, innate arousals to females, that are critical for evolutionary reproductive success, erupt and engulf the lives of young males.

At puberty male sexual arousal may be at its highest intensity, especially when the excitement is new, unexpected, and devastatingly joyous during the explosive, magical, overwhelming, most intense physical enjoyment ever experienced, orgasmic explosions. Pubescent boys are mesmerized by this remarkable orgasmic event that emerges in conjunction with, and as a result of, the equally amazing discovery that they are now locked into an automatic, uncontrollable, fascinating, maddening, omnipotent, intense, irresistible sexual arousal awakening when they gaze at an exquisite nude female, as personified by the Playboy centerfold playmate. Coming from a relatively calm pre-pubescent sexual environment dominated by their external world, males are now entering a pubertal milieu that is the antithesis of the past calm and complacency, a new sexual life that is ruled by an inner, uncontrollable intense sexual arousal produced when they are fortunate enough to view a gorgeous nude live female, and even more delightful if they can sexually interact with such a lovely fem fatal. The sadness and loss or happiness and good fortune drama's that unfold involving this perplexing but remarkable disposition to automatically and intensely respond with awesome, overwhelming delight when gazing upon, and/or physically connecting with, this magical, mystical form of a dream female, I propose, molds and shapes his current and future sexual development

An important possible outcome of the above sexual arousal scenario is the formation of a male predilection to be almost compelled to search for a predominantly physical sexual relationship with a female, a body connection rather than a mind connection. I believe that during puberty especially, and also continuing through adolescence and early adulthood, there is a stamping in, a potent conditioning, a major reinforcement via masturbation, sex with females and orgasm, of this bond between a male's instantaneous excitement when he looks at and physically connects with a desirable female. Orgasm acts as a fierce intoxicating reinforcement of this unconditioned reflexive bond (as compelling as the mighty reinforcement of food), repeated endlessly over and over again. I maintain that this uniquely male pubescent numerously repeated intensely enjoyed reinforcement of an innate unconditioned reflex that occurs when viewing and connecting physically with an appealing nude female, and continued unabated in adolescence and adulthood, leads to a compulsive disposition that typically forms the dominant motivational force in his relationships with females. Male intimacy with a woman is dominated by, or at least strongly influenced by, sexual gratification involving the excitement of viewing and physically interacting with a female. Non-sexual emotional and psychological bonding are of course part of a male-female relationship, but I am suggesting that a core foundation, and critically important motivation for males is there genetically ingrained, dramatically and relentlessly reinforced visual and physical arousal by female pulchritude. The force of this pervasive dominating male arousal and desire, fiercely imprinted and molded repeatedly, especially throughout puberty and adolescence, presents one of the most critical influential differences between males and females, and thus potential conflicts and problems in male-female relationships. (See "C. Intimacy" and "D. Male Sexuality and Female Sexuality" below for further discussion.)

5

Implications and Predictions.

A. MALE SEXUAL AROUSAL BY FEMALES AND MALE SEXUAL DESIRE FOR FEMALES.

The most important single aspect of the current theoretical model is that a male's view of an attractive nude female innately produces neurochemical reactions that are experienced as pleasurable and lead to sexual desire for this female. If and when sexual contact with this female occurs, the contact also produces automatic neurochemical reactions that are experienced as pleasurable. The following predictions are concerned with the male view of a naked female because this view is the basis, and only necessary component, of all male sexual arousals, including kinesthetic excitement from sexual contact with females.

Innate unconscious neurochemical sexual arousal is believed to remain stable over time, with neurochemical arousal levels commensurate with levels of female attractiveness. The perception of pleasurable feelings of sexual arousal is a conscious cognition that could be lowered or heightened by existing cognitions such as situational appraisal (Frijda, 1986), but I believe this perception of one's own arousal from the view and/or contact with a female is primarily powered by unconscious automatic neurochemical responses that under normal circumstances, in normally functioning males, are typically not consciously scrutinized, inhibited or distorted. It is extremely difficult, and perhaps impossible, to consciously modify the feelings of sexual arousal arising from neurochemical activation. In addition, males usually enjoy the feeling of sexual arousal and are inclined to accept and permit their inner arousal to occur. In an analogous manner we usually accept and permit pleasurable gustatory arousal to occur when we taste delicious food. Sexual desire, on the other hand, is a conscious cognitive wish which is reasonably stable because it is primarily determined by the level of arousal, but as a conscious wish is vulnerable to conditioning and learning, such as situational appraisal based on social (e.g., parents, females, peers, media, school, church) influences, and so less stable than arousal. The prediction is made that a positive environment will be associated with a higher correlation between male sexual arousal by, and male sexual desire for, females, then a negative environment. A positive environment would include the recognition, permission, support, and encouragement, availability and approval by females of male sexual arousal, including masturbation and orgasm, by, and male sexual desire for, attractive females by family, females, media, peers church, school etc. A negative environment would include negation, disparagement, prohibition, discouragement, punishment, unavailability and disapproval of male sexual arousal, including masturbation by, and male sexual desire for, attractive females by family, females, media, peers, church, school etc. The assumption is made that a positive or neutral environment would support or permit the natural innate association between arousal and desire to emerge and manifest itself. A negative environment, on the other hand, my act to decrease desire because of anxiety or guilt, for example, or tend to increase desire when frustration occurs. Under these negative conditions stable arousal, generally impervious to learning and or conditioning, would be associated with a more vulnerable, and so more variable, desire, which would reduce the correlation between arousal and desire. Under positive circumstances high arousal would be associated with high desire and low arousal would be paired with low desire. With negative situations high arousal may be associated with average desire because of guilt or anxiety or a strict superego. The role of male masturbation, sexual relations with females, and orgasm during puberty and adolescence in the experience of, and the associations between, sexual arousal and sexual desire, are significant and will be discussed below when sexual adjustment is considered.

Developmentally I believe that prior to puberty in early childhood there is little or low male sexual arousal by, and actual desire for, attractive nude female (Bancroft, 1983; Kinsey, 1948). Thus I predict very low correlations between arousal and desire prior to the onset of puberty. During puberty, on the other hand, the emergence of intense male sexual interest, activity and physical maturation (Bancroft, 1983) brings about, I propose, a very high correlation between male sexual arousal by, and male sexual desire for, attractive nude females. This very high correlation could be tempered or lowered if a negative sexual environment, effecting mostly desire, is present, as noted above. The high correlation between male sexual arousal by females and male sexual desire for females, especially under favorable environmental and experiential conditions, continues throughout male adolescents and adulthood, with a modest tapering off, but continuing high, during early and late adulthood.

B. MALE SEXUAL ADJUSTMENT AND MALE SEXUAL MALADJUSTMENT RELATED TO MALE SEXUAL AROUSAL BY AND MALE SEXUAL DESIRE FOR FEMALES DURING PUBERTY AND ADOLESCENCE.

Male Sexual Adjustment.

Under positive sexual environmental, attitudinal and experiential conditions, male sexual adjustment during puberty and adolescence, in relation to sexual arousal by, and sexual desire for, females is satisfactory and rewarding. Sexual arousal would result when males look at attractive nude females and when they achieved orgasms from masturbation and or sexual relations with females. With an inner and outer supportive sexual pubertal and adolescent milieu, males would be inclined to enhance their sexual pleasures by indulging themselves in masturbation and/or by having sex with females when sexually aroused by a fem fatale. Males would give themselves permission to be sexual. Males who are relaxed, happy and accepting of their sexual dispositions, such as being turned on by a scintillating seductress, by masturbation and by having sex with females, would most likely have the same positive sexual enhancing tendencies in their adult sexual relationships with women. Male sexual adjustment involves a male's proclivities to recognize, accept, gratify and rejoice in his sexual arousal by, and sexual desire for, lovely females, and of course *without causing harm in any way to anyone*, including himself. According to evolutionary design, ideal male sexual adjustment or fulfillment would occur when male sexual arousal, desire and sexual interaction with females were satisfied by attractive live females. In modern society this ideal evolutionary compulsion is typically not started or fulfilled until late puberty or early adolescence. During puberty and early adolescence sexual arousal, especially orgasm, and desire gratifications are frequently achieved by way of ideational representations, such as pictorial depictions, of appealing nude females via masturbation.

One vital contribution to successful pubertal and adolescent sexual adjust-ment is the experience of orgasm when masturbating and/or having sex with a female. Masturbation during these periods usually, and I suspect almost always, involves some idealized cognitive representation, view or touch, of an alluring female body (Kinsey, 1948). The experience of orgasm is an exceptional rein-forcement of the experienced intense arousal and the subsequent desire to extend and repeat this arousal. The role and impact of masturbation and orgasm for males during puberty and adolescence is, I believe, profoundly important. The pubescent boy discovers, usually unexpectedly perhaps, that he can experience, and rather easily, an indescribable, overwhelmingly exciting and gratifying physi-cal phenomenon that he could not have envisioned in his wildest dreams, an ecstatic explosive orgasm. Any verbal descriptions, or visual depiction that he may have heard, read about or seen, pale in comparison to his actual experienced mag-ical unparalleled delight. Such a phenomenal explosion that will remain, without doubt, the most intensely enjoyable physical experience that he will ever have, must, I contend, play some immensely significant role in his sexual life, and prob-ably non-sexual life. The delight that we experience when we taste delicious food, probably starting at birth, has the vital function of insuring our survival and is thus a critical evolutionary design. Mother nature selected individuals who enjoyed the taste of sweet fresh fruit and hated the taste of rancid, spoiled, rotting fruit. Enjoying the taste of delectable food, having our bodies exposed to com-fortable temperatures and breathing fresh air, are pleasures that we know will facilitated our well-being and are evolutionary designs to facilitate our survival. The experience of delight when viewing a gorgeous nude female and the ecstasy of orgasm based on the sight or thought and/or physical connection with a lovely nude female certainly enhances our pleasurable well-being, and I propose is the key evolutionary psychological mechanism that facilitates reproductive success. With so much riding on the success of this psychological mechanism, mainly the survival of the human race through successful gene transmission, mother nature guaranteed a positive outcome by incorporating through selection an unbeatable, incomparable, electrifying, best possible physical response, most intensely enjoy-able, most desired phenomenon of orgasm to solidify and bond a male's view of, and physical interaction with, a dream nude female. The rapture of being sexually alive (Campbell, 1988) is experienced most intensely through orgasmic explo-sions with a scintillating female. Perhaps the most intense and enjoyable physical rapture of being alive is the volcanic eruption of orgasm. Bottom line is that if males were not blown away, devastated, ecstatic when they gaze at a ravishing adorable female body, we all would not be here today. Mother nature absolutely insured our continued survival by selecting males who were repeatedly conditioned by the greatest of all physical delights, the experience of orgasm associated, and so stamped in, with the view of and connection with delectable females. I thus propose that the pubescent and adolescent recognition, acceptance, rejoicing in, having a sense of fulfillment and tranquility in the experience of striking excitement when viewing, thinking about and relating to devastatingly lovely females, coupled with the unimaginable, indescribably, intensely joyous experience of orgasm within this arousal and desire context, constitutes the core sexual foundation and optimum sexual adjustment for males.

Male Sexual Maladjustment.

Anxieties, guilt and conflicts surrounding masturbation, sex with females and orgasm, occurring within the context of sexual arousal and desire may interfere with, or detract from, the fulfillment of the critically vital evolutionary design of sexual arousal by, and sexual desire for, attractive (i.e., young, healthy, fertile) females, the necessary and only psychological mechanism devoted exclusively to facilitating reproduction. Under negative sexual environmental, attitudinal and experiential conditions, male sexual adjustment during puberty and adolescence, in relation to sexual arousal by, and sexual desire for, females is unsatisfactory and unrewarding. General sexual maladjustment would be reflected by a male who experiences conflicts, anxieties, guilt and depression about his sexual arousal by, and sexual desire for, females.

Some specifics sexual arousal dysfunctions are impotency, premature ejaculation and retarded ejaculation. Sexual dysfunctions that are due to physical causes that require medical attention are not considered here (see Kaplan, 1974). Hypo-arousal occurs in impotency and retarded ejaculation, while hyper-arousal takes place in premature ejaculation. Low male sexual desire for females may result from low male sexual arousal or from learning and conflicting interactions with females. In the arousal and desire disorders there should be an inquiry into what circumstances circumvented, inhibited, or in the case of premature ejaculation, excessively enhanced, the sexual arousal by, and sexual desire for, attractive females. Although excellent descriptions of etiology and treatment of the above sexual dysfunction has been presented (Bancroft, 1989; Kaplan, 1974, 1979; Masters & Johnson, 1970), little attention has been given to the sexual experiences related to sexual arousal and desire during puberty and adolescence as contributing etiological sources. My emphasis is that the most likely cause of male sexual dysfunctions can be found in an inquiry into pubertal and adolescent sexual experiences concerning sexual arousal and/or sexual desire experiences, with a focus on masturbation and orgasm. My contention is that male sexual arousal by delightful nude females, which leads to an intense desire to approach these beauties, erupts like a volcano around puberty because this manifestation is the sole innate perpetrator of gene transmission. When this remarkable event occurs, it's trials and tribulations during puberty and adolescence heralds in a basic sexual foundation that is well adjusted or maladjusted, that determines present and future sexual well-being or sexual maladjustment. I do not believe that much attention has been given to the consideration that puberty and adolescence may be the most critical periods for the development of male sexuality, including adjustment and maladjustment. I propose that if a male successfully copes with the sexual hurdles, challengers and personal transformations, within a generally positive sexual environment, he is most likely to be well adjusted sexually. Conversely, if a male does not cope successfully with the sexual trials, tribulations and personal sexual transformations within a generally negative sexual milieu, he is most likely to develop sexual dysfunctions and be generally maladjusted sexually.

If pubescent and adolescent males experience extreme anxiety, conflicts, inhibitions, guilt concerning their feelings of arousal, including intense arousals of orgasm, when they look at, think about, and/or physically interact with attractive females, they may be inclined to develop serious arousal problems in the form of impotency or retarded ejaculation. Males sometimes develop these dysfunctions during puberty or adolescence, but they are more likely to occur in adulthood (Kinsey, 1948). The more serious or disruptive problem is the greater shutdown of sexual arousal reflected in impotency. The anxiety surrounding the reaction of erection when looking at, thinking about, or relating to an alluring nude female most likely arises mainly from a negative sexual environment, although some negative influences could come from pre-pubertal negative sexual conditioning. Puberty, when arousal issues first become prominent, and early adolescence, may be critical periods for the formation of future potency problems. Guilt and anxiety about masturbation and/or sexual relations with females may be especially important in the creation of dispositions blocking this most obvious display of sexual excitement. Most cases of impotency occur after some period of potency (Kaplan, 1970), and I am proposing that anxiety and guilt about naturally experienced sexual arousal by females during puberty and adolescence may undermine the strength or potency of normal arousal.

Retarded ejaculation, where orgasm is terminated after successful erection, may be a less debilitating dysfunction than impotency and could result from a less severe negative environment during puberty and adolescence. Sexual arousal is experienced and enjoyed, but there is a block against the quintessential physical pleasure of orgasm, usually during sexual intercourse, and infrequently during masturbation as well (Kaplan, 1974). In retarded ejaculation male visual sexual arousal and kinesthetic sexual arousal by females are intact, but the culmination of the physical excitement, orgasm, is retarded. The causes of retarded ejaculation are probably multifaceted (Masters & Johnson, 1970; Kaplan, 1974), but one possible etiology might be a type of kinesthetic conditioning. Perhaps during puberty and adolescence a male masturbated up to the point of orgasm and then stopped before coming. The reason for stopping could be that he believed that penile stimulation was all right but climaxing, the ultimate and most significant expression of enjoyment, was not all right. If the male is guilty and anxious about his intense sexual arousal by females, orgasm is the focus and major expression of this excitement, and so if he does not come, he may think he is not having a real or meaningful sexual experience. Males may not have climaxed during sexual intercourse in order to avoid the risk of pregnancy. A male who had sexual interactions with a female such as sexual intercourse, penile stimulation, manual, body or oral contact up to but not including orgasm and ejaculation, may have conditioned himself to enjoy and accept arousal, but to reject or be anxious about climaxing. Thus, for various reasons, a male may have repeatedly engaged in sexual arousal activities, alone or with a female partner, but rarely or ever reached orgasm, which was responded to with anxiety if orgasm did occur. I propose that a male who masturbated or engaged in sexual relations with a female during puberty and adolescence up to the point of orgasm but rarely if ever climaxed, may be prone to perpetuate this practice, a practice that was deemed proper or safe or perhaps considerate for his female partner, in his future sexual experiences, and so a precursor of retarded ejaculation.

Low male sexual desire for females may be associated with low male sexual arousal by females or with various negative learning and environmental conditions that instill anxiety, guilt or conflict about male desire for females. If low desire is a reflection of, or occurs in conjunction with, low arousal to attractive females, one might suspect a low innate capacity to experience sexual arousal that may exist in 5% to 10% of the male population (Bancroft, 1989; Berenbaum et al., 1999), or the presence of negative environmental conditions that prevented normal high arousal. Sexual desire is almost always connected to sexual arousal, where the occurrence of arousal determines the occurrence of desire, the higher the arousal, the higher the desire. Sexual arousal is innate, automatic, neurochemically based, essentially unconscious and so extremely resistant to modification. In the case of impotency, such an arousal reduction does take place, but as noted above, probably under very toxic negative environmental and learning conditions during puberty and adolescence. Thus if low desire is associated with low arousal, the more likely cause of low arousal would be innate capacity or arousal occurring in 5% to 10% of the male population. More typically low desire occurs in conjunction with normal capacity for arousal (Kaplan, 1974), and here we would search for negative environmental learning that could have reduced the vulnerable conscious cognition of desire. Again, anxiety, conflict, strong superego and guilt about desire, fostered during puberty and adolescence, could have set the stage for low sexual desire.

In all arousal and desire dysfunctions one must consider the possible contribution of innate capacity to be sexually aroused. There is some evidence (Bancroft, 1989) that between 5% and 10% of the population have innate potential capacity for very high levels of pleasurable arousal, and I presume for sexual arousal, and that about 5% to 10% of the population are innately disposed to respond with very low levels of pleasurable sexual arousal. Some males who suffer from impotency, retarded ejaculation and low sexual desire may have these dysfunctions because they have very low innate capacity to respond sexually to attractive females. Some premature ejaculators may display this excitability because of their innate capacity to respond to nude females with very high level of arousal.

Another important consideration in arousal and desire maladjustment is the level of female attractiveness that males are responding to. When males look at, think about or relate to nude females who are not physically attractive they are not expected to be sexually aroused or to sexually desire these females. The occurrence of impotency, retarded ejaculation or low sexual desire under these circumstances would be natural, expected and not dysfunctional. If males respond with extremely high levels of sexual arousal to exceptionally gorgeous nude females, including premature ejaculation, such excitement would not indicate maladjustment.

Problems with male sexual *arousal* by attractive females are of paramount importance in almost all sexual maladjustments. The therapeutic goal for impotency, retarded ejaculation and low sexual desire is to increase sexual arousal by females, and to decrease sexual arousal in premature ejaculation. In general, sexual arousal will be increased when there is an increase in the perception of, and interaction with, more attractive nude females, and the removal of forces that block this perception. Sexual arousal will be decreased with decreased female beauty and those forces that counteract this excitement, such as anxiety, guilt, and frustrating circumstances. Male sexual desire will rise or fall with increases or decreases in sexual arousal. In dysfunctional males the automatic, innate association between sexual arousal and sexual desire is distorted and becomes mal-functional. Sex therapy has the task of discovering why nature's powerful design is not functioning. I propose that the source or foundation of male sexual malfunction reside in the anxiety, guilt, conflict and fear related to sexual arousal by, and thus sexual desire for, attractive, live, nude females, that occurs primarily during puberty and adolescence.

The number, intensity, and enjoyment of orgasmic experiences should be supported and encouraged in all sexually dysfunctional males, including premature ejaculators, and in all sexually well-adjusted males. In premature ejaculation, the length of arousal, full, intense and enjoyable orgasms are usually diminished, and these experiences need to be extended and increased. Reich (1973) believed that orgastic potency and gratification was the critical factor producing all types of psychological illness and happiness. He concluded that, "...those who are psychically ill need but one thing—complete and repeated genital gratification...the severity of every form of psychic illness is directly related to the severity of the genital disturbances" (p. 96.). Reich (1973) may have been wrong in his extreme, comprehensive, and overly simplistic emphasis that he attributed to the power of orgasmic release for the cure of mental illness and enhancement of mental health, but he was right on in recognizing the considerable importance of orgasmic arousal for elevating a sense of well-being, a crucial, natural, healthy evolutionary force vital for reproductive success, that has been all but totally ignored as a contribution to self-actualization. Reich (1973) was also ahead of this time in his focus on enhancing pleasure (i.e., hedonism) rather than the typical therapeutic approach of reducing pain (Freud, 1977). I find it unthinkable that anyone could question the value of partaking in what has to be for most, if not all, males, the quintessential physical delight. For me, the sense of exhilaration, ecstasy, self-actualization, well-being, and rapture of being alive is epitomized by my orgasmic enchantment.

C. SEXUAL IDENTITY, SEXUAL VARIETY, AND INTIMACY.

In addition to the influences of high sexual arousal (e.g., orgasm during masturbation and sexual interactions with females) during puberty and adolescence on sexual adjustment and maladjustment, these significant arousal experiences also effect variations in sexual identity, sexual arousal by a variety of females, and intimacy.

Sexual Identity.

Erickson (1950, 1968) placed particular emphasis on stage five of his eight stages of development occurring during puberty and adolescence, *identity versus identity confusion,* because he believed that what happens at this stage is of the utmost significance for adult personality, and that during this identity stage at puberty and adolescence the transition between childhood and adulthood takes place. A sense of identity, according to Erickson (1950, 1968), involves an inherent need to feel that one belongs to some particular or special kind of people, a set of values called "fidelity." "The person becomes aware of individual inherent characteristics, such as likes, dislikes, and anticipated goals of the future. This is a time in life when one wishes to define what one is at the present and what one wants to be in the future" (Hall, et al., 1998, p. 201).

During the identity stage, I believe, males establish their sexual identity. Male sexual identity, one aspect of the multifaceted overall sense of identity, is comprised primarily of recognition and acceptance of intensely pleasurable sexual arousal when viewing and relating to beautiful, nude females. Males identify with their erotic arousal by, and desire for, lovely females. Males see themselves as part of a vast number of males who respond to delightful females the same way they do, and believe they will certainly continue to respond this same way in the future. With a positive pre and post-puberty sexual environment, males will recognizes, accepts, enjoy and identify with their emerging fascination and excitement when viewing, relating to and experiencing delightful orgasms from masturbation and/or physical contact with intoxicating females. With inner and outer support, acceptance and freedom, males will go with their natural sexual flow and conceive of themselves as males who are pleased and content to be blown away by exquisite females, and who cherish the ecstasy of orgasm via masturbation or sexual contact with desired females. The quintessential physical joy of male orgasm experienced primarily because of, and in conjunction with, his enchantment with lovely female nude body's, repeatedly and passionately reinforces his identity as a sexual male obsessed by mesmerizing females who are responsible for, and the major contributor to, his orgasmic ecstasy, which makes him feel unbelievably fortunate to be a male. By saying "I am a male," he declares that he is predestined to have unfathomable ecstatic orgasmic adventures provoked and facilitated by ravishing females, a most glorious identity. If on the other hand, masturbation, sexual interaction with females, and orgasmic experiences associated with attractive females occurs within a negative environment during puberty and adolescence, fraught with guilt, frustration and anxiety, male sexual identity would be depressing, an estrangement, debilitating and represent *identity confusion* (Erikson, 1950). A positive sexual environment during puberty and adolescence would strengthen the bond between sexual arousal by, and sexual desire for, appealing females and so would also foster the sense of delight in sexual *physical intimacy* with females. Joyful orgasmic happenings with masturbation and especially sexual interludes with exciting females, probably occurring mostly in late adolescence, would reinforce the bonding of physical sexual intimacy with alluring females. The blissful thrill of orgasmic adventures that are not only associated with, but mainly produced by, a vision of, or interaction with, an enchanting nude female, forcefully orients males to desire this physical paradise in their relationships with gorgeous females. The most pleasure empowering feature of females is their ultimate capacity to facilitate a male's quintessential physical bliss of orgasm, and so male physical sexual intimacy becomes synonymous with orgasm. If masturbation, sexual relations with females and orgasmic occurrences during puberty and adolescence are riddled with anxiety, guilt, frustration and discomfort, then future physical sexual intimacy with females will probably be problematic and depressing rather than joyous. The physical sexual intimacy described above developed during puberty and especially late adolescence falls within stage five identity, and is different than the stage six intimacy (Erickson, 1950) presented below after Sexual Variety.

Sexual Variety.

If during puberty and adolescence, under favorable environmental circumstances, there is repeated male enjoyment of masturbation, sex with females and orgasm while thinking about, looking at and/or interacting with a *variety* of dazzling females, males will recognize, accept and repeatedly reinforce their automatic, innate proclivities to be sexually aroused by, and to sexually desire, beautiful females, *all* beautiful females. The evolutionary design of male sexual arousal and desire for, young, healthy, fertile females preordains males to be aroused and to desire all alluring females. Males are thus naturally promiscuous in their sexual arousal and desire temperaments, and orgasmic episodes repeatedly acknowledge and strengthen these deeply rooted inclinations. During puberty and adolescence intimacy for most males is reflected in their sexual excitement and desire for all gorgeous females, and this powerful innate predilection continues vigorously into adulthood (Symons, 1979).

Intimacy.

Young adults who mature successfully to stage six, *intimacy versus isolation*, according to Erickson (1950), are willing to unite their identity with others, seek partnerships, share in trusting relationships, love and care for someone as an adult rather than have adolescent infatuation, commit to a joint relationship, share in the rearing of their children and in the productivity of their relationships. The danger of the intimacy stage is isolation, which is the shunning of relationships because one is unwilling to commit oneself to intimacy (Hall, et al., 1998). The transition for males from sexual physical intimacy, established during stage five identity, that was restricted to striving for transitory, predominantly physical sexual intimacies, and searching for sexual identity based on sexual arousal by females, to stage six, *intimacy versus isolation*, may be difficult and problematic. Males need to restructure their predominant narcissistic orientation to be sexually excited by, and sexually drawn to, *all* attractive females, that is based on robust, automatic, innate predilection's originating in evolutionary selection, by incorporating a more altruistic, sharing, trusting, committed relationship with *one* female. Male sexual arousal and desire has to be focused on a single female. Males have to be emotionally aroused by a mutual sharing, caring, trusting and loving relationship, a partnership, I think, that is more natural and consistent with deeply ingrained female dispositions than with male inclinations, and thus could be a possible cause of problematic male-female relationships. Commitment in a loving relationship for males heralds the loss or reduction of sexual arousal, desire and fulfillment with a variety of females, a Herculean innate disposition, a change that is often difficult for males to achieve or adjust too. Mature non-sexual intimacy between a man and a woman, I believe, is analogous to the feelings a loving parent has for his or her children and grandchildren. Mature or ideal parental love for children and grandchildren involves intense joyous feelings when their offspring's experience happiness, especially when the parents or grandparents facilitated this joy. Loving parents and grandparents are fulfilled, rewarded, self-actualized, and overwhelmed with pleasure and pride (i.e., naches and kvelen) when their children and grandchildren are happy and healthy. Loving parents will do anything for their progeny, and are committed and devoted to their well-being. A quintessential delight of loving parents occurs when their children and grandchildren reciprocate their unconditional love. Mature intimacy and love between male and female adults, as inferred in Erickson's (1950) intimacy stage six, would include the characteristics of parent-offspring intimacy and love just noted. Males have been conditioned by sexual visual and kinesthetic intimacy pleasures by, and desires for, females, during puberty and adolescence, and they need to redirect, or incorporate into, their predominantly narcissistic and perceptual sexual arousals and desires, an excitement and joy derived from their knowledge that their female soul-mate is happy, healthy and self-actualized, and that they are dedicated and delighted to facilitate their female partner's well being. I would speculate that a very high number of males do not successfully realize mature adult intimacy because of their inordinately forceful innate sexual arousal by female pulchritude, which has been reinforced over and over again by their stunning orgasmic experiences during puberty and adolescence, which are primarily narcissistic sexual visual and kinesthetic arousals by, and desires for, females.

When reference is made to positive and negative environments above in regards to adjustment, identity, variety and intimacy, the following areas should be systematically and objectively evaluated in order to determine the specific and detailed nature of what constitutes positive or negative environments. Ideally, pubertal and adolescent males should be studied, and if possible, developmental studies following a given male from puberty through adolescence through adulthood should also be conducted. Only rough guidelines are given for the future construction of objective and reliable measurements of the areas suggested. 1. Frequency of sexual satisfaction in relation to looking at and or thinking about nude females, masturbation, having sex with females (e.g., intercourse, oral sex, petting). 2. Intensity of sexual satisfaction in relation to looking at and or thinking about nude females, masturbation, having sex with females (e.g., intercourse, oral sex, petting). 3. Frequency of sexual frustration, guilt, anxiety, depression in relation to looking at and or thinking about females, masturbation, having sex with females (e.g. intercourse, oral sex, petting). 4. Intensity of sexual frustration, guilt, anxiety, depression in relation to looking at and or thinking about females, masturbation, having sex with females (e.g. intercourse, oral sex, petting). 5. Frequency of masturbation, sex with females and orgasm, in general and at different ages. 6. Opportunities for looking at and or thinking about females, masturbation, having sex with females (e.g., intercourse, oral sex, petting). 7. Availability of pictorial, live or recalled images of nude females. 8. Level of beauty of viewed nude females. 9. Extent of nudity of females. 10. Conditions under which masturbation and sex with females occurred (e.g., intercourse, oral sex, petting). 11. Pre-puberty sexual experiences, environment, pleasures, anxieties and guilt.

D. Enhancement of Male Sexual Pleasurable Arousal.

A basic prerequisite that is needed to facilitate pleasurable male sexual arousal is for males to give themselves absolute, total, unquestionable, undeniable *permission* to delight in their sexual excitement when viewing and interacting with live, nude, lovely females (and again, and always, with the proviso that *nobody* is harmed in *any way*). I believe that heterosexual males have an inalienable right to bask in the glow of nude, live, female beauty. Males are entitled to the freedom of experiencing joy when they view the pulchritude of a gorgeous nude, live female. Being sexually excited by the sight and touch of such a female is a natural, normal, healthy, automatic male response that is innately programmed in male genetic structure, as this male arousal to females was critical in insuring reproductive success in our ancient for-fathers, and thus evolved as a necessary, normal, healthy pleasurable emotional response (i.e., a psychological mechanism) to insure the survival of mankind. My philosophy is that pleasurable male sexual arousal to the sight and touch of a beautiful female is a normal, natural, healthy, desirable, irrepressible, adventure to be cherished and celebrated. I contend that the most critical, fundamental, and necessary component of male sexuality is a male's delight in looking at a live, nude, lovely (i.e., young, healthy, fertile) female, and the central focus and purpose of this book is to understand and to celebrate this male sexual pleasure that ensues when he sees a gorgeous female. Male sexual arousal by females is a basic form of self-actualization that enhances mental and physical well being (Maslow, 1970; Reich, 1977). I believe that the focus in sexology should change from decreasing pathology (Freud, 1977; Kaplan, 1979; Masters & Johnson, 1970; Regan and Berscheid, 1999), a prevention focus (Higgins et al., 1999), to enhancing sexual self-actualization and sexual well being (Goldstein, 1939; Kahneman et al., 1999; Maslow, 1970; Rogers, 1961), a promotion focus (Higgins et al, 1999). Male sexual arousal, especially orgasm, is the quintessential physical experience of the "rapture of being alive" (Campbell, 1988), an experience that males are innately predisposed to enjoy and desire. The male orgasmic experience during sexual intercourse with a woman could be considered to be the culminating peak experience of the evolutionary goal to enhance reproductive success that started with a male's pleasurable sexual arousal by the sight of an enticing female. Reich (1973), who believed that orgasmic potency was the critical factor producing all types of psychological illness and happiness, concluded that, "...those who are psychically ill need but one thing-complete and repeated genital gratification..." (p. 96). This statement by Reich (1973) is an extreme oversimplification regarding mental illness, but it captures the potential considerable impact on well being of orgasmic experiences. Certainly the most enjoyable physical experience imaginable, an intense orgasmic explosion, perhaps one of the most crucial adaptation that mother-nature selected to guarantee gene transmission, second in importance only to a male's excitement when he views a gorgeous nude female, has to be a critical reinforcement component of any theory of male sexuality, and an enhancement of our psychological and physical well-being.

Male sexual arousal by females should be permitted to emerge naturally, without distractions, to achieve the highest levels of sexual excitement. Any thoughts other than the awareness of the visual perception of the female and the awareness of experienced sensation of arousal, could interfere with, and thus reduce, the level of felt sexual delight. Awareness of pleasurable perceptual arousals such as stimulating music and tantalizing smells may enhance overall excitement. Any thoughts, such as situational appraisal (Frijda, 1986) would tend to reduce the level of arousal. If there is a desire to prolong high levels of excitement, distracting thoughts could be a useful method of keeping arousal from reaching higher levels, such as orgasm in the practice of *Karezza* discussed below. In general, under normal conditions, however, thinking is the nemesis of powerful, innate, automatic sexual arousal. It is best to just go with the flow and let it emerge. It is like enjoying the taste of great food. Awareness of fine odors could be enhancing, but thoughts distract and diminish gustatory arousal.

Aging is a delight when you enjoy fine food. Aging is a delight when you enjoy great sex. Male sexual excitement by lovely females lasts as long as delight in consuming a fabulous meal. If real live nymphets are not available, for whatever reason, pictorial representation will do nicely (thank you). I am now 76 and happily enjoy real live beauties as well as my videos of these delightful enchantresses as much as I ever did in the past. If a male is healthy he can reap the benefits of his deeply rooted innate evolutionary designed capacity to experience intense ecstasy when looking at and/or having sex with pulchritudinous females for as long as he lives.

Although major emphasis has been given to the extremely important role of male visual arousal by females, a key player in mother nature's mission of facilitating reproductive success is of course a male's innate proclivities to be aroused by female tactile (i.e., intercourse, fellatio, touching, and body contact) stimulation leading to and including orgasm. The *Karezza* practice of India (i.e., *coitus reservatus*), where high levels of arousal are reached but orgasm is withheld, is one example of a marvelous way of prolonging the exquisite delight of the highest levels of male sexual arousal just prior to ejaculatory inevitability. During sexual arousal from intercourse, fellatio, hand or body stimulation, males can momentarily stop or change the ongoing stimulation and/or activity, reducing arousal and preventing orgasm, and then resume stimulating activity (a start-stop method), to a point close to ejaculatory inevitability, then stop again and repeat this process for periods of time enjoyable to a couple. This *Karezza* technique followed by orgasm is best employed within the context of a game called "master/slave" wherein each partner takes turns being totally selfish and self-indulgent (i.e., the "master"). One partner, the "master," is indulged in whatever manner he or she wishes with no concern for the pleasure of the giving partner (i.e., the "slave"), nor any guilt for being selfish. After the first partner has been spoiled in whatever way he/she wants to be, the situation is reversed and the slave becomes the master. This intoxicating playfulness opens the door for each partner to develop his/her skills at becoming a *dedicated student* of not only her/his partner's arousal needs and proclivities, but also an explorer into his/her own sexual capacities, predispositions, and turn-one's. A serendipitous rewarding consequence of becoming a dedicated student of your partner's sexual arousal needs is that when you succeed in pleasuring her/him, your partner is more likely to reciprocate and provide you with enormous gratification. If males and females want their sexual experiences to become more enchanting and ecstatic, I urge them to become dedicated students of their partner's sexual arousal proclivities and dedicate themselves to satisfying his/her erotic needs.

Because male visual arousal by females is so critical for male excitement, opportunities for male visual perception of females should be increased. Before, during, and after sexual encounters, arrange lighting, mirrors, angles, positions, activities were males can observe the finest, most attractive female characteristics. If women want to excite their male partner, they must show him their voluptuous, most curvaceous, most feminine, most youthful appearance. Looking at a lovely nude female is the primary, most potent and probably the only true male aphrodisiac, the ultimate "libido" source of male sexual arousal. The aphrodisiac that resides between male ears is not his mind or cognitions, it is his visual perception of females.

E. MALE SEXUALITY AND FEMALE SEXUALITY.

"In every age the battle of the sexes is largely a battle over sex"
(Symons, 1979, p. 262).

"...with respect to sexuality, there is a female human nature and a male human nature, and these natures are extraordinarily different....Men and women differ in their sexual natures because throughout the immensely long hunting and gathering phase of human evolutionary history the sexual desires and dispositions that were adaptive for either sex were for the other tickets to reproductive oblivion" (Symons, 1979, p. v). According to evolutionary psychology (Buss, 1989; 1994; & Symons, 1979), males desired young, healthy, fertile females in order to facilitate reproductive success, and females desired males with status who were willing and able to provide resources that would facilitate the survival of herself and her offspring. Males were selected who were sexually aroused by attractive (i.e., young, healthy, fertile) nude females, which reinforced the males desire to see and to have sexual intercourse with these attractive nude females, which facilitated reproductive success. Females were selected who were emotionally aroused by males with resources and status, which reinforced a females desire to have a committed relationship with this male who could provide resources that would enable her and her children to survive. In my opinion, the only major, extreme, and possibly absolute difference in male vs. female sexuality is that the evolutionary goal of female pleasurable arousal by male resources and status (a cognitive reaction), and desire for males (a cognitive reaction), is survival of self and offspring; while the evolutionary goal of male pleasurable sexual arousal by the attractiveness of females (a perceptual reaction), and sexual desire for females (a cognitive reaction), is reproductive success. The most distinctive and explicit male vs. female difference in sexual arousal and sexual desire occurs prior to physical sexual contact. Physical sexual arousal during kinesthetic contact (e.g., sexual intercourse, cunnilingus, fellatio, body and hand contact), including orgasm, appears to be similar for males and females. Males and females appear to have the same capacity to experience high levels of kinesthetic sexual excitement, including orgasm. During actual physical sexual interaction the intensity of sexual arousal and desire continue to be influenced by visual perception of females by males, and by cognitive evaluation of males by females, but direct kinesthetic excitement may be more, or equally influential in determining the levels of male and female physical sexual arousal. Female pleasurable emotional arousal by males prior to physical contact is produced by a complex, conscious, cognition involving the situational appraisal of her well-being (Frijida, 1986), in terms of male resources and status, which could be, and frequently is, influenced by learning and sundry environmental factors (Frijida, 1986). The female desire for a mate with status and resources, a complex conscious cognition, based on being aroused by a male with these qualities, could be strongly influenced by learning and the environment. Male pleasurable sexual arousal prior to physical contact is produced by the visual perception of an attractive nude female. Male sexual desire is primarily dependent on his visual perception of this nude female. Female "sexual" arousal by males and "sexual" desire for males prior to physical contact with males are more closely related to interpersonal social circumstances (i.e., male status and resources), rather than strictly sexual conditions (i.e., nudity, genital). Male sexual arousal and sexual desire prior to physical contact with females relate directly and strictly to sexual circumstances (i.e., nudity, genital). Female arousal is produced by cognitions about male resources and status, while male sexual arousal is produced by a perception of a nude female. Male physical arousal to the touch of a female (e.g., sexual intercourse, fellatio, body and hand contact) is primarily dependent on his visual perception of a nude female. Female physical arousal to the touch of a male (e.g., sexual intercourse, cunnilingus, body and hand contact) is primarily dependent on her cognitive appraisal of male qualities (e.g., caring, resources, consideration, personality, commitment), and by her cognitive appraisal of her own feelings and attitudes about a male (e.g., caring, interest, communication, sharing) and not on her visual perception of a nude male. I would say that females are emotionally aroused by their cognitions about a male's status and resources rather than, or less than, being sexually aroused by his naked body and genitals. Males know about the feeling of sexual arousal that occurs when they look at lovely nude females, but females can't know about, or experience this male feeling because females do not have comparable feelings of sexual arousal when they look at attractive nude males. Females know about the feeling of arousal that occurs when they think about males with status and resources, but males cannot know about, or experience this female feeling because males do not have a comparable feeling of arousal when they think about females with status and resources. The experience or feeling of arousal is probably qualitatively the same in males and females, produced by comparable unconscious neurochemical substrate (see Proposition 4 in Chapter 2), but I suspect the intensity of arousal is generally greater in males (because male perceptual arousal by females may be, on average, stronger than female cognitive arousal by males on average). The critical difference is that males are aroused by a visual perception of a nude female and females are aroused by a cognitive idea about a male's status and resources.

The evolutionary role of females is to secure the survival of herself and her off-spring's. To fulfill this role she is innately inclined to be emotionally aroused by a single male who could supply the economic resources and the psychological support, ideally of unconditional love, that insures commitment, and would guarantee the survival of herself and her children. One central component of unconditional love in a mature intimacy relationship is the dedication to, and the intense pleasure derived from, facilitating joy in others, as a parent may experience with his/her child and/or grandchild. The focus of females is on a relationship, the bonding with one male who will devote himself to her and their children. Most females grow up in an environment that supports their inclination to bond with a male in a committed loving relationship, and so her conditioning facilitates her ability to achieve an unconditional love affair with a male. The evolutionary role of males is to facilitate reproductive success via gene transmission. To fulfill this role males are innately disposed to be sexually aroused by all attractive females and so are inclined to have a sexual relationship with a wide variety of females. This male obsession is basically narcissistic, focuses on physical gratification and does not require commitment or an unconditional, loving relationship. A male's environmental conditioning is mixed but there tends to be a negative reaction toward his narcissistic promiscuous sexual inclinations with females, especially from females and especially so after marriage. The path to unconditional love is thus more problematic for males than for females. During puberty and adolescence young males may have doubts about their ability to love a female, and even their own future child, unconditionally, as described by Erikson (1950) in his intimacy stage, because males have only had the experience of being repeatedly and intensely sexually aroused by attractive females, with or without a relationship. Males have to progress from a basically narcissistic sexual arousal by, and desire for, attractive females, to a more mature, or certainly different, altruistic unconditional caring for the well-being of a female and/or their children. Males are compulsively driven by their sexual arousal and desire for all lovely females, which must be replaced by devotion to one female and to their children. Females are typically conditioned to want unconditional love from a male for herself and their children, and to be prepared to give a male her unconditional love in return, and are most likely more secure and confident than males in her ability to love unconditionally. Males have to modify, suppress, deny or make subservient their innate proclivity for promiscuity and substitute or develop a new orientation of mature love for a female, the kind of love he is probably capable of, or may have already developed for, his own child. Many males do achieve this more mature love for a partner or mate, but always within the context, and often confines, of his ever-present narcissistic disposition to be aroused by all attractive females, and his basic original orientation to be aroused by perceptual experiences rather than cognitions, such as altruism. Females, on the other hand, are emotionally aroused by cognitions, such as the recognition of a male's compassion, caring, considerateness, nurture, protection, generosity and status. Females do not have to give up or modify any different or less mature previous intimacy orientations with males. The resourcefulness, caring and commitment of a male can facilitate her mature reciprocal altruistic love. I suspect that females who have had a reasonably normal and positive relationship with their own parents, and were exposed to parents who displayed mature love for each other, could be disposed and capable of mature love with a male partner. Males who have had equally positive relationships with their parents are equally capable of mature love with a female partner, but they face the serious obstacle, or competing less mature orientation, of developing purely physical innate arousals to lovely female bodies, that is narcissistically dedicated to his own sexual pleasure, that distracts or may prevent the full development of more mature or unconditional love dedicated to the pleasure and well-being of his female mate and their children.

Based on the above evolutionary perspectives, female sexuality may differ from male sexuality in the following additional ways.

1. Males automatically, irrepressibly, and instantaneously at a specific given moment react with pleasurable sexual arousal to the sight of a live, nude, attractive female. Females do not necessarily react automatically, irrepressibly, and instantaneously at a specific given moment with pleasurable sexual arousal to the sight of an attractive nude male.

2. Males are sexually aroused by all attractive females and are thus predisposed to sexually desire a variety of such attractive female partners (e.g., promiscuity and prostitution). Females may be emotionally aroused by all high status, resourceful males, but they usually do not have sexual desires for a variety of such high status, resourceful males. Because a woman has a high level of parental involvement (Trivers, 1972), compared to a male, whose parental involvement could be measured in minutes (Trivers, 1972), and can thus afford to be promiscuous, a female needs only one male to secure assistance for her and her children's survival. (See Intimacy in section C above for a further analysis of possible male-female relationship problems that could occur when men are sexually aroused by a variety of females and women are sexually aroused by one male.).

3. The level or intensity of male sexual arousal to the sight of attractive females is usually very high, consistent, stable and predictable. The level of female emo-

tional arousal to the sight of high status, resource males, I would presume, is not as intense, consistent, stable and predictable, as a male's arousal to females. Males respond directly to the perceived female image. Females respond to their ideas about the resources of the perceived male image. Arousal based on cognitions (e.g., thinking about sweet fresh fruit, males thinking about a live nude female), are more vulnerable to learning and environmental influences than arousal based on direct perceptions (e.g., enjoying the taste of sweet fresh fruit, males pleasure in looking at a live nude female). This difference in the intensity of arousal also contributes to the tendency of males to want a greater variety of sexual partners than females do.

4. The activation of neurochemical substrate (see Proposition 4 in Chapter 2) in males in response to their perceptions of a nude female is probably more powerful and direct than the neurochemical activation of females in their response to the cognition of male resources and status. Pleasurable arousal to eating tasty food is probably more powerful and direct than pleasurable arousal while thinking about tasty food.

5. Males are more concerned sexually with a female's physical appearance. Females are more concerned emotionally with a male's behavior (e.g., resources, status, love, consideration, empathy, communication).

6. Males are turned off by the sight and touch of nude males. Females do not appear to be turned off by the sight and touch of nude females.

7. Male history of orgasmic arousal is unique, including nocturnal emissions starting around puberty, long continuous history of masturbation, ease of achieving orgasm through masturbation, repeated experiences of intense orgasms (Kinsey, 1948). The continuous and frequent reinforcement of intensely pleasurable orgasmic experiences enhance the importance and desirability of achieving orgasm, especially by contact with females, where the physical and psychological pleasure is the most intense. The history of female orgasmic experiences is not comparable to male orgasmic history (Kinsey, 1946) and I believe is not as important to achieve or as necessary for females as it is for males.

8. Most males are sexually aroused by the sight or image of attractive females almost every day, for the major part of their lives. Most females, I suspect, are not as pervasively and continuously aroused by the sight or image of attractive males. In addition, the pursuit of pornography, promiscuity and prostitution are typically male dominated (Kinsey, 1964; Symons, 1979).

9. Most males experience frustration and discomfort when sexual gratification, especially the experience of orgasm with an attractive female, does not occur, the longer the delay, the greater the disappointment and discomfort. I do not think

females have as intense a need, especially for orgasm, or are as intensely disappointed and uncomfortable as males are, when sexual frustration occurs.

10. For males there is a critical period of sexual development that occurs during puberty and adolescence, when a basic foundation and structure consisting of male sexual arousal by, and sexual desire for, attractive nude females, emerges because of an evolutionary design. Females may, or may not, have a critical period when arousal, based on the concept of male resources, emerges following an evolutionary design.

11. A male is attracted to physical qualities in a female that are most different than his physical make-up. A female is attracted to cognitive qualities (e.g., commitment, compassion, consideration, nurturance, succorance) that are most like her own cognitions.

12. Female emotional arousal by the idea of male resources is a cognition concerning resources that are similar to arousals produced by other cognitions. Male sexual arousal by females is based on a visual perception of a nude female body and is different than other arousals because genital arousal occurs in response to looking at a nude female. Female arousal is based on an idea and male arousal is based on a perception. Males can easily understand a female's arousal to an idea about male resources as males have arousals about ideas also. Females, however, do not have the experience of being genitally aroused by the view of a naked male and so do not "know" what the feeling of male sexual arousal is like. Female desire for males is based on a pleasurable arousal by an idea. Male desire for females is based on a pleasurable arousal by a perception.

13. Male sexual arousal by a female diminishes significantly when he does not see a nude female. Female desire for a male probably does not diminish when she does not see a nude male.

14. Male pleasurable sexual arousal by attractive nude female bodies is produced by relatively *simple*, clear cut, unambiguous, automatic, innate reactions to visual stimuli, and remain fairly stable and consistent from puberty through adulthood. The vision directly produces the arousal and no cognitions are necessary. The cognitive awareness of the arousal feeling occurs when the automatic neurochemical activation takes place when the female body is viewed, and is necessary for the production of the ensuing sexual desire for the female. Female pleasurable arousal by resourceful and committed males is produced by a *complex* set of cognitions concerning the nature of resourcefulness and what constitutes being committed, which has considerable variability at different female ages and with different female learning experiences in different social settings, within and between female.

Females and males appear to be alike in their sexual arousal during actual sexual interactions (i.e., intercourse, cunnilingus, fellatio, hand and body contact), as far as derived physical enjoyment. Most males and females enjoy high levels of physical arousal and orgasm from kinesthetic stimulation. Males and females are probably also similar in their enjoyment of masturbation. The major difference is on the heavy reliance on male visual arousal by females in determining male physical sexual excitement.

Because of the considerable and significant female-male differences in their sexuality, and because it is extremely difficult, and perhaps impossible, for males to "know" or empathize with the experiential feelings of women, and vice versa, I maintain that insights and understanding of male sexuality must come from males, and insights and understanding of female sexuality, used for building theoretical models, must come from females. I can not "comprehend," empathize with, "know," feel the female *experiences* of menstruation, gestation, lactation, orgasm and sexual arousal. The theoretical models of human sexuality that attempt to apply the same principles to males and females (Regan & Berscheid, 1999), suggesting there are no male-female differences in sexuality, are most unlikely to be correct. In actual sexual experiences, males must learn from females what they want, need and experience, and females must learn from males what they want, need and experience, if the considerable differences are to be understood and capitalized on. The critical importance of communication between couples stressed by Masters and Johnson (1966) is strongly supported. Hopefully differences can be used for excitement and variety rather than frustration and disappointment (see Enhancement of Male Sexual Pleasurable Arousal in this chapter).

General theories of personality (Hall et al., 1998) that rely heavily on social-cultural learning and development may be appropriate and accurate for both males and females. Theoretical models of sexuality, however, should recognize the vast male-female differences, certainly from the evolutionary perspective presented in this book, and construct distinct and unique models for males and for females. I want to stress that male and female sexuality are *different* from each other and not in any way superior or more inferior to each other (Symons, 1979). The view advanced by Symons (1979) is "…that selection has produced marked sex differences in sexuality—implies that neither sex can be usefully considered to be merely a defective version of the other" (p. 4).

F. MALE SEXUAL ORIENTATION.

The contention of my theoretical model is that the ultimate foundation and cause of male heterosexuality is the innate predisposition to react with pleasurable sexual arousal to the sight of a live, nude, young, healthy fertile female, a disposition that evolved in order to facilitate reproductive success. I propose that the crucial proximal cause of male sexual arousal by the sight of an attractive nude female is genetically programmed. In my own research on male and female homosexuality (Siegelman, 1972 a, b, 1974 a, b, 1978, 1979, 1981 a, b) I found that for a sizable number of normal, none-clinical male and female homosexuals in the U.S. and England, homosexuals did not differ on parent-child relationships or on adjustment/mental health in comparison to non-clinical normal male and female heterosexuals. To the best of my knowledge, there still does not exist any convincing evidence that homosexuals have different developmental experiences, including parent-child interactions, that are significantly different from the development of heterosexuals, nor that homosexuals are less well adjusted than heterosexuals. It appears to me that male homosexuality is as deeply ingrained, automatic, intractable and irrepressible as male heterosexuality. I thus *speculate* that there is probably a genetic basis for male homosexuality (Bailey, Dunne & Martin, 2000), just as I propose that there is a genetic basis for male heterosexuality, but it is important to point out that there is no convincing evidence to support my assumption that male heterosexuality and male homosexuality are genetically determined (Huffman, 2002). Male homosexuals may possess a unique and different genetic structure than male heterosexuals. The proximal causes of male homosexuality and male heterosexuality are proposed to be genetic, but the research evidence to date is at best equivocal (Huffman, 2002). The ultimate cause of male heterosexuality is proposed to be evolutionary selection, and the ultimate cause of male homosexuality is currently unknown.

G. SEX RESEARCH CONTENT, DESIGN AND METHODOLOGY.

Sex Research Content.

Very little research has been devoted to male sexual arousal by females (Janssen, 2002; Rosen & Beck, 1988), what I consider to be the defining and central issue in male sexuality, and the focus of this book. For post-pubertal males, I believe, the most critical and influential foundation of their sex life is their sexual arousal when they see, think about or have sex with females. All other areas of sexalogical research on males pale in comparison to the frequency, significance, influence and joy of male sexual arousal by, and desire for, beautiful females. Male sexual arousal to the sight, idea and touch of an enchanting female, including the remarkably scintillating quintessential physical delight of orgasm, is a prime example of the rapture of being alive (Campbell, 1988). It is thus perplexing that sexologists have neglected this crucial and fundamental area of male sexual arousal and desire for females. We have never attempted to systematically study the nature, significance and influence of joyful sex. I think that sexual excitement should be the central mission of sexalogical research, and yet it is all but ignored. Sexologists give considerable attention to reducing anxiety and discomfort but ignore the facilitation of joy, a prevention focus rather than a promotion focus (see Proposition 6 in chapter 2). Could sex researchers be uncomfortable, or think that their subjects would be uneasy, when exploring very personal, usually unrevealed sexual activities such as sexual intercourse, masturbation, fellatio, frequent sexual arousals by, and desires for, females, despite the pioneering work of Kinsey (1974)? Is male arousal by enticing Playboy centerfold type females consider to be an obvious truism that does not need to be studied in depth by sexologists? Are research grant proposals on intimate sexual behavior not submitted because of anticipated rejection? Do we lack the methodology, beyond penile tumescence, to evaluate sexual arousal? Are sexologists more concerned with social issues like AID's, disorders, deviations, precise animal or physiological studies than with understanding the nature, significance and enhancement of sexual joy? Is information obtained from males about how they are turned on by gorgeous females thought to be too subjective and unreliable? Probably all of the above to various degrees

Male sexual arousal by, and sexual desire for, lovely nude females defines male sexuality as a discipline, and distinguishes this domain from all other disciplines. The bulk of research in sexology could be subsumed under, or has considerable overlap with, other areas of investigation such as sociology, physiology, medicine, comparative psychology, psychopathology, anthropology and education,. It seems to me that the essence and core of male sexology that is of the greatest relevance and concern to the overwhelming majority of males, is the particular structure, function and development of normal male sexual arousal by, and sexual desire for, females. Male sexual arousal and desire for females, with its significant evolutionary roots, is one of the main justifications for considering sexology a separate and unique science. Another primary innate perceptual arousal, with the evolutionary design to support survival, has received mind-boggling attention and consumption, namely enjoying the taste of delicious food. Male rejoicing in the sight and touch of beautiful females is certainly as important as food, as this male proclivity has been responsible for perpetuating life on this planet for millions of years, and yet this remarkable sexual phenomenon has been relegated to the back burner by sexologists. Increasing delicious gustatory arousal and desire is universally worshiped. What about supporting and increasing the bliss of male sexual arousal by females?

Sex Research Design and Methodology.

Because of the great important that I place on male sexual experiences during puberty and adolescence, and on the impact of these experiences on later sexual behavior, developmental research will be required, despite the difficulties of doing such studies. Ideally the same males should be evaluated during puberty, adolescence and adulthood. Operational definitions and precise measurements must be devised for the evaluation of positive sexual environments and negative sexual environments to replace the crude general descriptions that I noted above. Actual sexual behavior, such as a male looking at a female, should be directly observed in the moment and evaluated at that moment, with objective tests (e.g., neurochemical reactions), rather than examine recollections, thoughts or only paper and pencil tests. Ideally real, live, nude females should be used, but in studies involving pubertal and adolescent males, such models could probably not be utilized, and so pictorial representations might be used as a substitute. I propose that the most important measurement in male sexology is the precise evaluation of the level of male sexual arousal (e.g., neurochemical activation) in response to precise levels of female attractiveness (see Female Attractiveness Scale in Chapter 3), used to see whether or not there is a high positive correlation between level of female beauty and level of male arousal. This measurement is the definitive foundation of male heterosexual behavior, and is the major, and perhaps the only, association that is *unique* to sexology, and thus distinguishes sexology from all other disciplines. This relationship also appears to be the only psychological mechanism devoted exclusively to facilitating gene transmission.

Subjective introspection may be the best method for gaining *initial* insight into the sexual arousal of males by attractive nude females. Socialization includes the process of learning about existing social-cultural information, an internalization of external data. The predominant focus of education is on cognitions such as knowledge, beliefs and attitudes. In contrast to such ideas, there is the world of feelings, emotions and sensory perceptions, all of which are experienced primarily through subject introspection. Science generally favors ideas and objective observable data as a source for uncovering the mysteries of life. A virtually unexplored phenomenon that captured my imagination was the feeling that I could access only through looking inward, my sexual arousal to lovely nude females. Such introspections are usually frowned upon by the scientific community, but it was clear to me that my subjective feelings of excitement produced by lovely females was the foundation, and the *only necessary* component of my sexuality, the emotion that dominated and directed all significant aspects of my sexual life, the introspection that subsequently formed the central dynamic of my conceptual framework of male sexuality. This book is an outgrowth of my life-long probing into my own sexuality. Although subjective introspection is of paramount importance, and perhaps the only way to gauge how significant an experienced emotion is in the life of an individual, the scientific method with precise objective methodology must always be used, in addition, to support or refute concepts and conclusions derived from introspections, which I have attempted to do in this book (see especially Propositions 4 and 5 in Chapter 2).

6

Conceptual Framework of General Emotional Hedonic Arousal and Cognitive Desire, Innate Male Sexual Arousal by Females and Non-Sexual Male Behavior, and New Directions.

Figure III below depicts a proposed general conceptual framework of emotional hedonic arousal and cognitive desire applicable to all males and females. One exception of course is male sexual arousal and desire as outlined in Figure II in Chapter 4, which is unique for males. Figure III depicts a "general theory of behavior" (Hall et al., 1998, p. 17). A "Generalized Proposition" in Figure III is a Proposition applied to all perceptual arousals under "A" and "B" (i.e., visual, gustatory, kinesthetic, auditory and olfactory) for males and females, and to all cognitive arousals under "C" for males and females. A Generalized Proposition in Figure III, for example Generalized Proposition 3, relates to Proposition 3 "A" in Figure III, incorporates the model presented in Figure II in Chapter 4, which outlined male sexual perceptual emotional arousal by females and male sexual desire for females, a unique configuration for heterosexual males, as well as all other primary perceptual arousals and desires. Secondary perceptual arousals noted under "B" in Figure III involve perceptual arousals that are produced by learned cognitions (e.g., situational appraisal) rather than innate predispositions that are present in "A." Cognitive arousal depicted under "C" in Figure III includes arousals from ideas rather than perceptions and are learned rather than innate. Responses of primary perceptual arousal "A" probably start at birth and are dominant or primary during the first year or two, except for male sexual arousal by females that starts around puberty. Secondary perceptual arousals under "B" may become more prominent in early childhood. Cognitive arousals probably become more pervasive from later childhood through adulthood. With the exception of male sexual arousal by females, which starts with intensity around puberty, the behavioral developments in "A" are a foundation for the behavioral developments in "B," and the "A" and "B" foundations continue to operate and influence the behavioral developments in "C." Primary perceptual arousals and primary cognitive desires are more nomothetic (i.e., groups are studied and people are compared on the same concepts). Secondary and cognitive arousals and desires tend to be ideographic (i.e., individuals are studied one at a time without making comparisons to other people). I would agree with Allport (1937) who argued for a personality theory that combines nomothetic methodology, which is purported to be more typical of the natural sciences, with idiographic methodology, said to be more representative of the social sciences. I believe, and hope, that my theory is a rapprochement between the natural and social sciences.

FIGURE III. CONCEPTUAL FRAMEWORK OF GENERAL EMOTIONAL HEDONIC AROUSAL AND COGNITIVE DESIRE.

A. Primary Innate Perceptual Emotional Hedonic Arousal (Evolutionary, Genetic, Universal, Nomothetic) and Cognitive Desire. Generalized Propositions 1 and 2.*	B. Secondary Perceptual Emotional Hedonic Arousal (Idiographic Unique, Social/Cultural) and Cognitive Desire.	C. Cognitive Emotional Hedonic Arousal (Idiographic,Unique, Social/Cultural) and Cognitive Desire.
Primary visual, gustatory, kinesthetic, auditory and olfactory stimuli (e.g., nude female, fresh fruit, rotten fruit, spiders). A state, in the moment perception. Generalized Proposition 4.	Secondary visual, gustatory, kinesthetic, auditory and olfactory stimuli (e.g., great art, music; graffiti, hard rock). A state, in the moment perception.	Conscious ideas, thoughts about self, others and the milieu (e.g., thoughts about sex, family, culture, society). A state and/or trait, ongoing, continuous ideas.
Arousal capacity and unconscious neurochemical personality traits (EI and SS). Generalized Proposition 10.	Arousal capacity, unconscious neurochemical personality traits (EI and SS). and situational appraisal.	Arousal capacity, unconscious neurochemical personality traits (EI and SS) and situational appraisal.
Unconscious neurochemical, autonomic, somatic and behavioral responses. Generalized Propositions 4 and 5.	Unconscious neurochemical, autonomic, somatic and behavioral responses.	Unconscious neurochemical, autonomic, somatic and behavioral responses.
Action dispositions: Preparation for approach or avoidance actions. Generalized Proposition 3.	Action dispositions: Preparation for approach or avoidance actions.	Action dispositions: Preparation for approach or avoidance actions.
Situational appraisal. Generalized Proposition 10.		
Conscious and/or unconscious motivation by hedonic feelings (e.g., joy or fear). Generalized Proposition 6.	Conscious and/or unconscious motivation by hedonic feelings (e.g., joy or fear).	Conscious and/or unconscious motivation by hedonic feelings (e.g., joy or fear).
Conscious and/or unconscious desire to continue or stop, to approach or avoid persons, situations, or ideas. Generalized Propositions 8 and 9.	Conscious and/or unconscious desire to continue or stop, to approach or avoid persons, situations, or ideas.	Conscious and/or unconscious desire to continue or stop, to approach or avoid persons, situations, or ideas.

---

* Propositions 1–10 can be found in Chapter 2.

All pleasurable primary innate perceptual arousals are automatic, instantaneous, universal, enhance and perpetuate life (i.e., evolutionary dispositions), and reflect Rousseau's (1762/1993) proclamation that natural man at birth is good (see Proposition 6 in Chapter 2 for a detailed discussion). Rousseau (1762/1993) also noted that what is natural or inborn at birth is often corrupted by his environment, which I propose starts with secondary perceptual arousals and desires presented under "B" in Figure III, and reaches its full potential for "corruption" with cognitive arousals and desires shown under "C" in Figure III. There may be a transition from predominantly life enhancing experiences in primary innate perceptual arousals and desires under "A" to the greatest potential for both life enhancing and life threatening experiences during cognitive arousal and desire under "C." Primary perceptual innate desires are more subject to cognitive learning than primary innate arousal, and so these desires may lead to positive and negative life experience. The enjoyment of sweet, fresh fruit is life enhancing, but the desire to eat too much or too little food, even healthy food, can be life threatening. Enjoying innate pleasurable arousals that occur, for example, when you eat fresh sweet fruit, or when males look at lovely nude females, are usually healthy and enhancing because such arousals typically lead to desires that facilitate survival and procreation, and because the arousal experience itself is usually a wonderful physical rapture of being alive. Pleasurable emotional perceptual arousal feelings, especially enjoyable innate perceptual arousals, are almost always beneficial for the person having these perceptual experiences. Secondary perceptual arousals presented under "B" in Figure III represent wide latitudes for experiencing pleasurable arousals. Perceptual experiences would include playing musical instruments, viewing or constructing art, sundry vocational activities. Under normal circumstances it is probably fairly easy to avoid unpleasant secondary perceptual arousal experience. Secondary perceptual arousals are determined primarily by conscious cognitions produced by environmental learning and so are unique to each individual's idiosyncratic developmental environment. Cognitive arousals under "C" in Figure III probably represent the greatest variation in individual differences, within a person and between persons. Cognitive ideas that are arousing and lead to likes and dislikes often change over time for any given individual. Personal perception of art, music, sports are relatively stable over time. Personal ideas about self, family, government and sex are less consistent over time.

A major paradigm depicted in Figure III is that hedonic emotional arousal is the central motivational force that determines desire. Desire, instinct, drive or need is the central component of many theories of personality (Hall et al., 1998). The paradigm in Figure III presents a personality theory that proposes that emotional hedonic arousal is the major determinant of personality structure, function and development. Hedonic arousal is fundamentally the experience of pleasure or pain and operates to extend and repeat pleasure, and to stop and avoid pain (see Proposition 6 in Chapter 2). Hedonic emotional arousal, I suggest, is the primary motivational force that underlies the structure, function and development of personality. Under "A" primary innate perceptual emotional arousal, we approach or avoid those innate perceptual experiences that are pleasurable or painful. Under "B" secondary perceptual emotional hedonic arousal, and "C" cognitive emotional hedonic arousal, we approach or avoid those learned perceptual or cognitive experiences that are pleasurable or painful. The structure, function and development of personality are dependent upon pleasant and unpleasant emotional experiences, or more simply, upon the *law of effect* (see Proposition 6 in Chapter 2). If we ask the question, "Why do we have certain desires and aversions?" The most parsimonious, and I believe reasonable, answer is that we desire what we have experienced as pleasurable, and that we avoid what we have experiences as painful. I agree with Zajonc (1998) who notes that, "...emotional phenomenon enter into almost every aspect of social life...and it can be readily argued that of all major psychological processes, the emotions are of prime importance" (p. 591). I thus propose that pleasant and unpleasant emotions are the basic motivational foundation of almost all behavior, and certainly in the formation of personality, as expressed through various desires or needs.

An important assumption underlying the paradigm presented in Figure III is that we are innately oriented to enjoy certain types of perceptual stimulation (i.e., "A" in Figure III), and when we experience these emotional arousals we seek to extend and to repeat them. When we taste great food, bask in delightful climate, hear soothing sounds, enjoy visual and kinesthetic sexual ecstasies, we hope these experiences will go on for ever, and be repeated *ad infinitum*. Tension, anxiety, pain and death ensue if these enjoyable life sustaining and gene transmitting emotional experiences do not occur. Mother nature (or evolutionary design if you prefer) has hard-wired these pleasurable reactions in the nervous system in order to facilitate survival and reproductive success. The goal of evolutionary design, then, is to enhance, improve and intensify pleasurable emotional arousals that support life and gene transmission. This natural support of pleasure is incompatible or inconsistent with Freud's (1920/1965) pleasure principle, the principle of tension reduction by which the id operates. Tension reduction occurs when, "...the behavior of a person is activated by internal irritants and subsides as soon as an appropriate action removes or diminishes the irritation (Hall et al., 1998, p. 40). The aim of an instinct is to return the person to a prior state that existed before the instinct appeared, one of relative quiescence. Freud presents a conflict model of motivation where behavior is driven by unconscious biologically based instinctual urges that demand gratification. An inborn instinctual need for food stems from bodily excitation, a condition of nutritional deficit in the tissues of the body. The inborn psychological representation of this hunger instinct is a wish for food. If gratification of this hunger instinct is blocked by social or other environmental constraints, behavioral compromises occur that focus on substitutions or symbolic representations of the originally desired object. In contrast to Freud, I propose that we are born with innate predispositions to enjoy the taste of certain kinds of food, such as fresh sweet fruit, and *after* we have such an enjoyable gustatory experience we are automatically inclined to consciously and/or unconsciously desire the pleasure to continue and to desire to approach and repeat the pleasurable object and/or experience (see Figure III in Chapter 6). If the pleasure of eating is accompanied by a reduction in hunger discomfort, then the desire to continue and repeat the pleasurable eating activity is further reinforce and thus increased. Desire for food occurs only if pleasure is first experienced when tasting that food, and the developed inclination is to extend, increase and repeat the pleasure. Evolutionary design that supports life and reproductive success has programmed humans to enjoy our innate life-supporting perceptual arousals, and to stop and avoid painful experiences that do not support life and gene transmission. The evolutionary model of encouraging and capitalizing on increasing pleasurable excitement also does not agree with Murray's (1938) regressive need tension reduction theory, where the force of a need acts to reduce or terminate an existing unsatisfying situation. I agree with Campbell (1988) that the primary goal of life is to seek and perpetuate the "rapture of being alive." I am also pleased by the musical refrain "accentuate the positive and eliminate the negative."

The conscious awareness of pleasant and unpleasant emotional hedonic arousals provides the major driving force or motivation for behavior, in particular the desire to approach or avoid objects and/or situations. Hedonic arousal, I propose, is the major life force and energy that directs almost all human behavior (Higgins, 1997). I would define hedonism as the experiencing of pleasurable emotional arousal in a certain situation or activity, that typically leads to a desire to continue and to repeat this pleasurable experience in similar situations or activities; and as the experiencing of painful emotional arousals in a certain situation or activity, that typically leads to a desire to stop this painful experience and to avoid this experience in similar situations or activities. The basic concept of hedonism is essentially the same as Thorndike's (1930) *law of effect*, and synonymous with the concept of pleasant and unpleasant emotions (see Proposition 3, and especially Lang, 1995 and Zajonc, 1998). I propose that hedonism is the primary energy source, the life force and basic motivation of evolutionary design. When we experience the emotions of pleasure and pain, probably from birth onwards, we innately want the pleasure to continue and the pain to stop. Hedonism, for example, is the basic energy source for innate perceptual emotional arousals (see Figure III "A" above). There are five innate perceptual emotional arousals, visual, gustatory, kinesthetic, auditory and olfactory. Pleasurable arousal of these five senses by pleasant sights, like attractive nude females, tasty food, comfortable temperatures and enjoyable sounds and smells, support life and survival. Painful sensory arousal, like extreme cold or heat and starvation can cause death. We are thus born with innate predispositions to enjoy certain types of stimulation, like pleasant weather and the taste of sweet fresh fruit, which are healthy and necessary for our survival. There is one other innate perceptual pleasurable emotional arousal, a male's enjoyable sexual excitement in response to looking at, and having sex with, attractive nude females, which begins around puberty. In contrast to the five innate perceptual senses that begin to respond at birth and are devoted to survival, male sexual arousal by females, starting around puberty, is uniquely dedicated to facilitating reproductive success. The experiencing of pleasure and pain in all innate perceptual arousals orients the individual to extend and to desire the same pleasurable arousal again, and to reduce and avoid any experienced pain. Experiencing pleasure from the five innate perceptual emotional arousals carries out the evolutionary design of supporting life and facilitating reproductive success. Pleasure and pain derived through the five innate perceptual emotional arousals most poignantly reflect, I believe, what Campbell (1988) believed we are all seeking, the actual feeling of the rapture of being alive, "...so that our life experiences on the purely physical plane will have resonance within our own innermost being and reality..."(Campbell, 1988, p.3). Smothermon (1980) notes that, "Truth is not what you believe but what you experience directly..." (p. 13), and I would say that emotional arousal experiences via the five innate perceptual modalities reflect this "truth." Innate perceptual emotional arousals, in addition, may be part of what Jung (1953/1978) called the collective unconscious, a universal "...psychic residue of human evolutionary development..." (Hall et al., 1998, p. 85, and see Proposition 1 above). Hedonism, I propose, is the basic energy source that motivates most of our behavior. Pleasure attracts in certain situations and activities, and pain detracts in certain situations and activities. This hedonistic principle also operates in secondary perceptual emotional cognitive arousal and in cognitive emotional arousal (see figure III "B" and "C" above). Although hedonistic feelings, such as joy or fear, are usually experienced as conscious cognitions, especially in primary innate perceptual arousals, unconscious pleasurable and painful emotional reactions certainly occur and could influence behavior. Defense mechanisms (A. Freud, 1946), for example, may operate unconsciously to distort reality and so modify pleasurable and painful feelings and their impact on behavior.

I consider primary innate perceptually emotional hedonic arousal to be the most basic and critical life support system, and for males, includes the most important, universal and unique enhancement of reproductive success via gene transmission (i.e., "A" in Figure III). The male psychological mechanism of sexual arousal by attractive females that leads to sexual desire for these females, constitutes a unique and singular psychological mechanism devoted exclusively to the facilitation of reproductive success. I thus believe that primary innate perceptual emotional hedonic arousals, such as the enjoyment of tasting sweet, fresh fruit, or the male delight of looking at a lovely nude female, are natural, necessary, genuine, "true," as well as beneficial, good and the desirable. These innate perceptual arousals, that are predominantly unconscious, usually lead to conscious desires (i.e., for sweet fresh fruit, for attractive females) that are also beneficial and desirable. Conscious desires, however, may be, and usually are, influenced by sundry conscious cognitions, such as situational appraisal (see Proposition 10 in Chapter 2), which modify, or perhaps "corrupt," the desire. The means used to satisfy these desires emanating from innate perceptual arousals are influenced predominantly by conscious ideas (under "B" and especially "C" in Figure III) that may lead to healthy, positive outcomes, or unhealthy, negative consequences. I propose that primary innate perceptual arousals form the necessary foundation and motivational base for the formation of certain personality traits expressed as desires or needs. The most important innate perceptual hedonic arousal, for the formation of male personality traits, is male sexual arousal by lovely nude females. This male psychological mechanism, that includes sexual desire for alluring females, produced by male sexual arousal, that emerges with intensity at puberty, may also contribute to the formation of identity and autonomy, morality and prejudice, to be discussed below. All other primary innate perceptual hedonics arousals, that function at birth and onwards, may significantly influence the Erikson (1950) stage of basic trust versus basic mistrust during infancy, when there is oral-respiratory and sensory-kinesthetic (i.e., incorporative modes) emotional hedonic arousals; and also the early childhood stage of autonomy versus shame and doubt, where there is anal-urethral and muscular (i.e., retentive-eliminative) emotional hedonic arousals. I propose that the development of the infant sense of basic trust versus basic mistrust, and the formation of autonomy versus shame and doubt during early childhood, are the product of the innate disposition to extend and enjoy pleasurable perceptual stimuli, and to end and avoid unpleasant perceptual stimuli (i.e., innate hedonic arousals noted under "A" in Figure III). Secondary perceptual emotional hedonic arousals (i.e., "B" in Figure III) are strongly influenced by environmental learning (e.g., situational appraisal) and contribute to the formation of unique individualistic perceptual desires and aversions. Although secondary hedonic perceptual arousals are unique for each individual, there are frequently large numbers of people who enjoy, or do not enjoy, certain types of music, food, art, sports, literature etc. Cognitive emotional hedonic arousals (i.e., "C" in Figure III) are produced by ideas based on environmental learning and represent the most unique configuration of traits and cognitions that distinguish individuals from each other. The developmental learning environment is different for every person and so a person's ideas, attitudes, and intensity of acceptance or rejection of cognitions, tend to be unique to that individual. Some ideas, however, such as religious concepts and beliefs, are fairly uniform for large numbers of individuals.

RELATION BETWEEN INNATE MALE SEXUAL AROUSAL BY FEMALES AND NON-SEXUAL BEHAVIOR.

We inherit dispositions to respond with pleasurable arousal or with painful arousal to specific primary innate perceptual stimuli (i.e., visual, respiratory, kinesthetic, auditory and olfactory), in order to facilitate survival or reproductive success (under "A" in Figure III). These inherent dispositions are called psychological mechanisms. Primary perceptual stimuli are stimuli that elicit arousals and desires that are necessary for survival and reproductive success. Pleasurable primary innate arousal typically produces the desire to continue and to repeat the pleasurable arousal. Extreme pleasurable arousal (e.g., orgasm) almost always leads to the desire to continue and to repeat the experienced arousal. Painful primary innate arousal typically produces the desire to end the painful feeling and to avoid experiencing the painful arousal again. Extreme painful arousal (e.g., burning pain from hot flame) almost always leads to a desire to end and to avoid the painful arousal. There is only one psychological mechanism that is devoted exclusively to reproductive success, a male's sexual arousal by, and subsequent sexual desire for, attractive nude females. Gene transmission via reproductive success is the central and most important mission of evolutionary design. What males specifically inherit are automatic pleasurable sexual arousal responses when they look at a lovely nude female. Males do not inherit a desire to look at, or have sexual contact with, a lovely nude female. Male inherit the disposition to *respond* with pleasurable arousal when they view attractive nude females, which typically leads to, or produces, a cognitive conscious desire to continue, to look again, and to approach the lovely nude female. This male desire occurs only if arousal occurs. Arousal occurs only if a male sees an attractive female. Cognitive desire can be influenced by sundry other cognitions. Visual arousal is influenced primarily by level of female beauty. The arousal reaction is unconscious (e.g., neurochemical activation). The desire is conscious. Arousal is the driving force and energy than direct the course of desire, but conscious desire can be influenced by other cognitions (e.g., situational appraisal), but arousal is overwhelmingly directed by the perception of the female image. Thus the most important aspect and the basic foundation of male sexuality is his sexual *arousal* by his vision of a lovely nude female. The only psychological mechanism devoted exclusively to facilitating gene transmission is powered by a male's arousal by the sight of lovely females. This male sexual arousal by females, which includes achieving orgasmic delights, is the most intensely enjoyable physical experience of all the innate pleasurable perceptual arousals noted under "A" in Figure III above. Male sexual arousal by females is also unique in that it is the only perceptual arousal that is a response to a human figure, the female body, rather than to inanimate objects, such as food, air and sounds. Evolutionary design has selected those males who enjoy the most intensely ecstatic arousals by females because this arousal is the central, and I believe the only, force in an innate psychological mechanism that promises to be successful in gene transmission through reproductive success. This powerful male sexual arousal by beautiful females does not occur in males with intensity until around puberty.

I suggest that the amount and degree of male pleasure-pain, satisfaction-frustration, concern-indifference, conflict-conflict resolution, control-impulsivity, inhibition-disinhibition associated with his experiences of sexual arousal by attractive females during puberty and adolescence may impact on some behavioral aspects of his non-sexual development. I propose that the sexual odyssey of pubertal and adolescent males urgent, exciting, maddening erotic arousals, with their deep evolutionary roots, could influence their non-sexual behavioral development. I propose that the emergence and development of innate male sexual arousal by females during puberty and adolescence influences the development of non-sexual behavior, such as personality, identity and autonomy, morality and prejudice.

PERSONALITY: AESTHETICISM, CURIOSITY, VARIETY AND NOVELTY.

Aestheticism.

When males perceive graceful, harmonious, symmetrical, elegant, delicate, curvaceous ravishing female bodies that takes their breath away during puberty and adolescence, do they subsequently delight in viewing, thinking about, or creating other graceful, harmonious, elegant, beautiful objects, places, activities and ideas? The male who rejoices in viewing incredibly gorgeous nude female bodies may be predisposed to be thrilled by other rhapsodic perceptions and ideas, such as photographic gems, great artistic creations, wonderful musical performances, exceptional literary works and the wonders of nature, like fantastic sunsets, flowers and landscapes. Being mesmerized by great beauty may motivate some males to create original works of art, music, literature, and to understand and preserve nature's glorious creations.

Curiosity.

The female body is mysterious and not only different for most males. Around puberty males are extremely curious to observe the fascinating body of a dazzling nude female. Previous curiosity about the environment and oneself existed, of course, but nothing as mesmerizing and exciting as a lovely female body. Does male sexual arousal by females, starting around puberty, that entails the perception of females as different, mysterious, unknown, enigmatic produce in males an excitement about this female enigma, lead to the disposition to discover, to be curious about what is unknown or perplexing in life, in science, relationships, the arts, vocations, religion, etc., where the intensity and nature of the pubertal resolution of this sexual mystery predispose males to be curious and inquisitive, to different degrees, in these sundry life experiences? Could the foundation and prototype of male curiosity about the unknown enigmas of life in general be shaped and developed by his inquisitiveness and beguilement by the wondrously unfathomable female form? When a male's curiosity about females is pleasurably satisfied by views and contact with lovely female bodies, he may also be intensely pleasurable aroused, if fortunate enough, by exhilarating orgasmic delights. Males who are thus rewarded by their curiosity about females may be inclined to see, or anticipate, such enjoyment if they satisfy their curiosity about other environmental situations and conditions, such as science, the arts, vocations, religion, nature.

Variety and Novelty.

Males are aroused by a variety of females, all females who are young, healthy and fertile. Males are especially excited when they see and/or experience sex with a new, unknown, novel attractive female. If the male has enjoyable sexual experiences during puberty and adolescence with a variety of females, he may be inclined to seek pleasures in a variety of new and different life experiences, such as visiting new places, tasting new foods, reading about, and relating to, different people or places and open to new ideas and activities. Males who have a limited number of pleasurable experiences with relatively few attractive females, or generally unpleasant sexual experiences with different females during puberty and adolescence, may not be interested in seeking pleasures in a variety of new and different activities and situations. Males who recognize, accept, support and encourage their delights in seeing and relating to gorgeous females may also find pleasure in novel, different, unique and various activities, objects, places, people and ideas. Creative thinking reflecting original, unique and innovative ideas may be more pronounced in males who comfortably enjoyed female variety and novelty during puberty and adolescence. The creation of original art, music and literature may also be produced by males who were titillated by a wide variety of charming females. New and unknown lovely females are perceived not only as different, but as mysterious and exotic by males. Does this fascination with the mysterious enchantress that a male desperately wants to know about, discover, probe, explore form a foundation or disposition to decipher the unknowns of science, art and nature? Does the innate and powerful disposition of males to be sexually enchanted by a variety of different females, starting with intensity around puberty, contribute to, or predispose a male to appreciate, enjoy, produce and create variety, novelty and originality? I would predict that males who are anxious and guilty about their sexual arousal by delightful females, who submit to social pressures to deny and abandon these luxurious experiences during puberty and adolescence, would be more inclined to pursue more conforming, plebian, uncreative, less original and less provocative activities and vocations. Males who acknowledge, accept, identify with, are secure with and are prideful of their loving, unbiased, autonomous joy of viewing, interacting with, and curiosity about, a wide variety of different enchanting, mysterious, exotic, gorgeous females, are more likely to be mesmerized by, and creative innovators in, artistic, scientific and vocational endeavors that have similar propensities and qualities. Could the development of aestheticism, curiosity, variety and novelty dispositions, as noted above, be related to the disproportionate number of renowned and prominent males (as opposed to females) natural and social scientists, artists, musical composers, literary author, photographers, educators and explorers?

IDENTITY AND AUTONOMY.

Male sexual identity that develops during puberty and adolescence that involves recognition, acceptance, self-respect and exultation for intense sexual arousal by beautiful females, which may have encountered various degrees of resistance, opposition and derogation from environmental sources, such as family, church, media and especially females, reflects an independent and autonomous orientation. The declaration that I am a male arousal machine and I am happy and proud to manifest this obsession is a declaration of independence and autonomy despite possible oppositional environmental pressure. Males who securely recognize who they really are sexually, even when external forces include pressures to change and modify this self-image, are probably generally oriented to be, and to perceive themselves as, independent and autonomous in their non-sexual thinking and behavior, which reflects their identification as masculine males. If a male, on the other hand, feels anxious and guilty about his constant and intense sexual arousal by scintillating females, because of social pressures that devalue and derogate his obsessive sexual arousal by all attractive females as being amoral, immature and narcissistic, he is displaying social dependence and conformity. These males may feel insecure and ambivalent about their sexual identity and identity as males because of the conflict between their inner sexual arousals and desire and there ideas about being responsible and proper males. Males with a sexual identity that involves a submission to social demands may also recognize and manifests dependent and conforming dispositions in their non-sexual activities and interactions. A basic foundation for the development of autonomy may be formed during early childhood (Erikson, 1950).

Morality.

If males follow their evolutionary instincts during puberty and adolescence, they would make love not war, protect and not destroy, impregnate and produce new life. The purpose and goal of male sexual arousal by females is to make love, babies, and experience quintessential physical joy and usually to make females happy. His goal is to make love and be loved. Males ideally want females to want them, to want to make love to them in as intense and passionate a manner as they passionately want to make love to a female. These are males with fundamentally and naturally good intentions, who will become adults with good intentions if environmental conditions and learning support their innate morally positive orientations. As Rousseau (1762/1993) said, "Everything is good as it leaves the hands of the author of things, everything degenerates in the hands of man" (p. 5). The "author of thing," I maintain is evolutionary design.

Male innate predispositions, such as enjoying food, pleasant temperature, the views of attractive nude females and tranquil sounds are narcissistic, selfish emotional arousals that facilitate survival and reproductive success. If males encounter little resistance or opposition from females and societal pressure in their predilection for sexual arousal by females, these males will devote their energies and resources to experiencing as much sexual pleasure as possible. Resistance or opposition by females and society to curb and restrict male sexual arousal by females, and female and social pressures to have males commit to monogamous relationships and take responsibility for their children, will force males to suppress or modify their innate sexual arousal orientations. Unbridled male sexual arousal may lead to a proliferation of single female parenting and male unlawful behavior to get money to pay females for their sexual services, which describes the life scenario that is frequently played out among young, lower class, urban males and females in our society. When females and society successfully control and restrict male inclinations to be aroused by, and so desire, all lovely females, males tend to accept a committed monogamous relationship and their parental role and curb their narcissistic promiscuous appetites, which is the typical case among middle and upper class young males and females. What constitutes positive and healthy evolutionary designs, male sexual arousal by all attractive females, may lead to various outcomes depending on environmental conditions, especially female permission or restriction. The evolutionary design itself, of male sexual arousal by females, is a positive manifestation of the critical and singular function of reproductive success and focuses on making love, being in love, hoping for reciprocal love, the raptures of pleasurable physical ecstasy, the creation of life (one critical altruistic aspect that is not narcissistic). The goal of gene transmission that is achieved primarily by male sexual arousal by females is perhaps the most important positive and desirable objective of mankind. This psychological mechanism, male sexual arousal by females, that appears to be the most important and only mechanism devoted exclusively to facilitating reproductive success, and thus the primary and essential determinant of our existence on this planet, must be intrinsically good, valuable, necessary and high in moral value. Now the goal of male sexual arousal by females, which is natural, moral and necessary, may be "corrupted," as Rousseau (1762/1993) implied by societal pressures, conditioning and learning. When males rape females, abandon their children, commit crimes to get money to pay for female sexual favors, there is a corruption of the means to achieving the positive ends of procreation. The essential goal of male sexual arousal by females is laudatory, moral and required, but the road to achieving this innate objective may be fraught with amorality, crimes, conflict, discord; or it may be paved with altruism, morality, tranquility, commitment, mature love and self-actualization, depending on environmental conditions and learning.

Prejudice.

Males are innately, automatically, and unconditionally aroused by all gorgeous female bodies. All lovely females, irrespective of race, skin color, nationality, religion and all other identifying characteristics, are perceived by males as exciting and desirable. Male vision is innately unbiased and non-prejudicial in response to female pulchritude. Male neurochemical response (see Proposition 4 in Chapter 2) to all marvelous nude females is instantaneous, automatic, unconscious and uniform. During puberty and adolescence, males who recognize, accept and identify with their lack of prejudice when sexually responding to female bodies may also manifest a generally unbiased attitude when perceiving the race, skin color, nationality, religion, etc. of all individuals. Of course unbiased natural visual arousal to females can "…degenerates in the hands of man" (Rousseau, 1762/ 1979, p. 5). Man's natural "instinctive" arousal disposition can be distorted and corrupted by his environment. If males follow the path of their inborn natural arousal to all lovely females, they are more inclined, circumstances permitting, to be less prejudicial in terms of the race, skin color, nationality and religion of the people they relate to.

NEW DIRECTIONS.

Theories of sexual behavior involving psychological processes, and perhaps all psychological theories of behavior, are incomplete, and may also be incorrect, if they do not include or consider the following characteristics. (1). An explanation of *why* a given proposed behavior occurs. Personality theories (Hall et. al., 1998) present descriptions of behavior, for example a taxonomy of needs or traits (Eysenck, 1976; Murray et. al., 1938), or developmental stages (Erikson, 1950; Freud, 1920/1965), and some theorists propose explanations of how the needs, traits and developmental stages are formed (Hall et. al., 1998). Freud (1920/ 1965), for example, presents a complex and elaborate structure of personality development which depicts how personality structures are derived. I know of no personality theory, however, that explains *why* a proposed need or trait or developmental stage occurs. Evolutionary psychology (Buss, 1994; Symons, 1979) is the only theoretical approach that I know of that proposes an answer (see Propositions 1 and 2 in Chapter 2). Thus I propose that male sexual arousal by lovely females (a personality trait) is driven by hedonic sexual excitement (i.e., how this psychological mechanism functions) *because* of the evolutionary design to facilitate reproductive success (i.e., why this psychological mechanism exists). (2). A recognition of the probable motivational influence of hedonic emotional arousal as presented in Proposition 2 and 3 in Chapter 2 on personality development and structure. There is robust evidence (Hall et. al., 1998; Higgins 1997) that supports the motivational or reinforcement process of Thorndike's (1935) *law of affect*, or more precisely Skinner's (1953) *empirical law of effect* as expressed by emotional reactions (see Proposition 3 in Chapter 2) that influence the formation of personality. One theoretical approach that recognizes sexual arousal as an emotional response is presented by Everaerd, Laan, Both and Springer (2001), where relevant stimuli that produce an emotional response can activate approach behavior. Their conception of sexual arousal being an emotional reaction (Lang, 1995) is consistent with my model of hedonic emotional arousal presented in Proposition 3 in Chapter 2. I thus propose that emotional hedonics arousal in males by females is the primary motivational reinforcement source of male sexual desire for females (see Propositions 3 and 6 in Chapter 2). (3). A focus on normally functioning individuals if the theory purports to explain normally functioning individuals. There is a strong tradition in psychology, beginning with Freud (1920/ 1965) to study clinical patients and then make generalizations about normal or non-clinical populations (Hall et. al., 1998). There has been an overemphasis in psychology and sexology to study psychopathology rather than normal behavior (see Proposition 6 in Chapter 2). Early studies of clinical patient homosexual subjects led to the conclusion that all homosexuals were neurotic and had pathological early parent-child relationships (Siegelman, 1972 a, 1974 a, 1987). My work on non-clinical, normally functioning homosexuals, revealed no significant differences in the adjustment and parental background of male and female homosexuals versus heterosexual (Siegelman, 1978, 1979, 1981a, 1981b, 1987). I thus propose that insight into male sexual behavior must be based on normal, non-clinical samples of male heterosexuals. I believe that a better understanding of the dynamics of normal heterosexual male functioning will facilitate greater understanding of pathological heterosexual male behavior, rather than vice versa (see "Male Sexual Adjustment and Maladjustment in Chapter 5). The joy and sense of well being experienced in normal male sexual experiences is consistent with the evolutionary design that considers male sexual ecstasy with females to be an innate, positive, beneficial and necessary goal for the achievement of reproductive success. The examination of normally functioning males who experience great sexual satisfaction is certainly the best source for discovering how best to enhance sexual delights. The continued study of sexual psychopathology is certainly necessary, but, in addition, we must greatly increase our efforts to understand and improve the joy of normal male sexual experiences. (4). A recognition that male sexuality is unique and different from female sexuality (see "E. Male Sexuality and Female Sexuality in Chapter 5). The critical difference, of course, is the core dynamic that orchestrates male sexuality, his excitement when he sees a gorgeous nude female, starting around puberty. I thus propose separate and distinct theoretical models for male sexuality and for female sexuality. (5). Distinguishes between sexual arousal by, and sexual desire for, females, and describes the relationship between sexual arousal and sexual desire, where hedonic sexual arousal is the key motivational force underlining male sexual behavior, and most importantly, male sexual desire (see Proposition 8 and "A. Male Sexual Arousal by Females and Male Sexual Desire for Females" in Chapter 5 and number 8 under "Major Principles" in Chapter 4). Although the major emphasis of my theoretical orientation has been on male sexual arousal by females, the evolutionary design of facilitating gene transmission can be accomplished only if arousal leads to sexual desire for females. I thus propose that a clear distinction must be made between male sexual arousal and desire, which has not been presented thus far in past research. (6). A recognition of the critical importance of puberty and adolescence in the development of male sexuality (see "Puberty and Adolescence" in Chapter 4). The significance of the influences and consequences of male sexual arousal by, and male sexual desire for, females during puberty and adolescence has not been adequately examined. I propose in depth and longitudinal studies of male pubertal and adolescent sexual arousals and desires for females be conducted, with an emphasis on how sexual arousals are dealt with. Puberty may be an especially important period for sexual development and I believe we know very little about sexual feelings (i.e., pleasures, anxieties, frustrations), attitudes, trials and tribulations and consequences of pubescent boys sexual experiences in relation to females. (7). Includes precise physiological measurements underlying sexual behavior, and precise measurements of environmental stimuli (e.g., nude females, people, objects). In addition, state, in the moment, real, normally experienced behavior should be examined (see Proposition 11 in Chapter 3). When Skinner (1953) presented his *empirical law of effect* insisting on direct observation of overt behavior as opposed to Thorndike's (1935) *law of effect*, which referred to subjective descriptions of satisfying and unsatisfying effects, there were no precise measurements of pleasant and unpleasant emotional reactions. Today however, we can accurately evaluate emotional responses with tools like left prefrontal cortex activation (Davidson, 1994), startle reflex (Lang, 1995) and the *Duchenne smile* (Ekman, 1993) (see Proposition 11 in Chapter 3). I propose that the emotional response of sexual arousal should be evaluated by precise valid and reliable instruments, and ideally in an environment that closely resembles or actually is, a, real, live typical behavioral experiences (see Proposition 3 in Chapter 2).

The five primary innate perceptual arousals (see "A" in Figure III above) may represent the foundation of pleasurable and painful emotional experiences that support the evolutionary design of enhancing reproductive success. Primary innate perceptual arousals support survival through pain reduction (e.g., reduced hunger discomfort), via the pleasurable experience of eating tasty food. A reduction of pain, a prevention focus (Higgins, 1997), and an increase of pleasure, a promotion focus (Higgins, 1997), contribute to, and are necessary for, survival, which in turn is necessary for reproductive success. Probably the highest levels of health and well being are achieved by those individuals who experience the greatest number of innate pleasurable emotional arousals, because evolutionary design supports pleasurable reinforcements, such as the "rapture of being alive" (Campbell, 1988). The primary innate perceptual arousal, devoted exclusively to facilitating gene transmission, male sexual arousal by females, is powered predominantly by pleasurable excitement, a promotion focus (Higgins, 1997). Effective gene transmission is most efficiently accomplished when males experience high levels of sexual delight when they see and interact with lovely females. As noted above, the best levels of health and well being are probably achieved by those males who experience the most pleasurable emotional sexual arousal by females. Here the incentive or basic motivational force of evolutionary design is the experience, both conscious and unconscious, of ecstatic male sexual arousal by lovely females. Evolutionary design then is founded on, and is successful when, people experience pleasurable emotional reactions. We are addicted and innately oriented, through our five hereditary hedonic perceptual arousals, to enjoy what is good for us, because it supports life and reproductive success, and what is beneficial for us, because it enhances our physical and mental well being. We automatically strive to experience as many innate pleasant arousals as we can. Life is driven by a hedonic emotional force to increase and extend the raptures of being alive. I am presenting a theory that optimistically celebrates the innate pre-dilections of evolutionary goals to support life and facilitate reproductive success, goals that can be achieved when innate perceptual pleasurable arousals occur. I don't know of any other psychological theory that has an intrinsic basic foundation that supports and celebrates, and deems necessary for survival and reproduction, the experience of sexual pleasure for males, as well as general pleasure (i.e., five innate perceptual arousals) for males and females.

Sex is great fun! We should do research on the most central aspect of sexual behavior which is the experiencing of ecstatic perceptual and orgasmic responses during male-female sexual interactions. We have not examined high levels of sexual arousal. Perhaps the only necessary component of heterosexual sexual behavior is the excitement experienced during sexual encounters (e.g., intercourse, oral sex, petting) between males and females. We have not explored the magical world of sexual bliss, except physiologically (Masters & Johnson, 1966). Sex is not only about physiology. Sex is primarily about having some of the most remarkably enchanting and quintessential physical arousals imaginable. I believe studies in sexology should be directed more to the essence and core of sexology, the joyous delights of sexual interaction between males and females. My theory about male sexual arousal by gorgeous females is directly concerned with the delirious and mesmerizing male excitement that is generated when he connects sexually, visually and/or physically, with a lovely female. Could it be possible that nobody has conducted research on the nature of one of life's greatest pleasures? Unfortunately, yes! At the other end of the continuum there is mind-boggling interest in getting to know every there is to know about the taste of delicious food, another one of the five innate perceptual arousals. In retrospect, I think I might have been originally drawn to the field of sexology because I thought it would be fascinating to study about what was such a joyous and exciting part of my life. I was also motivated to develop the theory presented in this book because the question I posed to myself many years ago was, "What turns me on sexually?" My answer, a beautiful nude female, looking and having sex with her. The nature of my turn on, my arousal and delights with beautiful females, was always of interest and concern for me, as knowing possible answers would help me make my sexual adventures more enjoyable for me and my girlfriend. I propose that we must do research on what sex is primarily all about, the joyous rapture of being sexually alive.

The most unique and most import dynamic of my theoretical approach, as summarized in Figure II in Chapter 4, and Figures III in Chapter 6, is that hedonic emotional arousal, or simply *the law of effect* (Thorndike, 1932), is the primary and exclusive driving force, energizer, motivational impetus for almost all human behavior. Pleasant and unpleasant emotional arousals produce inclinations to extend and replicate the pleasurable experiences and to stop and avoid the unpleasant experiences. From birth to death this hedonic principal orchestrates all of our significant ideas and behaviors. In the present book I have focused on the evolutionary design involving male sexual arousal by attractive females, were the key element is male emotional *arousal*. To the best of my knowledge, I do not know of any theoretical orientation (Bancroft, 1989;Berscheid & Reiss, 1998; Hall et al., 1998; Rosen & Beck, 1988) that considers emotional hedonic arousal as the central dynamic of their theory. In addition, there is no theory that uses emotional hedonic arousal as the fundamental dynamic within an evolutionary design framework, as depicted under "A" in Figure III, Chapter 6. I believe there has been a reluctance by researchers to examine or speculate about unobservable, subjective, internal emotional experiences (Zajonc, 1998). There has only recently emerged an interest in evolutionary social psychology (Buss, 1987, 1989), and even more recently in evolutionary psychology related to sexology (Allgeier & Wiederman, 1990). The precise measurement of neurochemical, somatic, autonomic and behavioral activation underlying emotional responses (see Propositions 4 and 5 in Chapter 2) related to the perception of sexual stimuli is still in its infancy. The methodology of evaluating in the moment state reaction to precisely delineated external stimuli, such as male reacting to a nude female, has not been constructed (and looms of course as a major shortcoming and challenge for the model presented in this book, although guidelines have been presented in Proposition 11 Chapter 3). The major research emphasis on pathology (see Proposition 4 in Chapter 2) must change, or include a major focus on the understanding and improvement of normal, healthy, joyous sexual experiences. I believe that a better understanding of normal, healthy, joyous sexuality, as presented in this book, will be the key to greater insight into sexual psychopathology (see section "B" in Chapter 5). The critical importance of puberty and adolescence for the structure, function and development of male sexuality has not been recognized or explored. I propose that as sexologists we must think "outside of the box," and consider theoretical and methodological approaches that are especially germane, useful and reasonable for the unique domain of studying male sexual behavior, and perhaps sexual behavior in general, as far as considering hedonic emotional arousal as the basic motivational source. I hope that I have presented a theoretical research model that will be useful in understanding and facilitating the joyous rapture of being sexually alive.

The thesis of this book is that mother nature insured reproductive success by selecting males with the capacity and predisposition to experience the "rapture of being alive" (Campbell, 1988) when they viewed and had sex with lovely females. Male sexual joy in this context is a celebration of life. Certainly a greater understanding of the nature of male sexual joy that celebrates life should be a major task for sexology, and should constitute a field that I would call *Evolutionary Hedonic Sexology* (EHS), which encourages insight, appreciation and the enhancement of male and female sexual excitement. EHS, in terms of the present book, is distinctive in its emphasis on instantaneous, pleasurable, differential male arousal (based on dedicated neurochemical substrate) by, and desire for, different levels of real, live, nude female beauty. EHS is thus *uniquely* defined by male sexual arousal and desire. EHS is of course dedicated to a celebration of female, as well as male, sexual joy. The focus of this book is male sexuality because it evolved, in part, from my intense life-long curiosity about, and devotion to, my own sexuality, which has been comprehensible to me as a joyous, emotional, arousal experience in response to lovely females. Only women, I believe, can know and understand their sexual arousal to, and sexual desire for, men. Women must lead in understanding and insights that will facilitate appreciation and enhancement of female sexual joy. The research goal of hedonic psychology is to maximize human happiness (Kahneman, 1999). The research objective of EHS is to maximize human sexual happiness. Evolutionary psychology, according to Cosmides, Tooby, and Barkow (1992), is psychology that is informed by knowledge gleaned from evolutionary biology. *Evolutionary Hedonic Sexology* is sexology as informed by evolutionary psychology (Buss, 1994; Cosmides et al.; Symons, 1979) and by hedonic psychology (Kahneman et al., 1995).

References

Abercrombie, H. C., Schaefer, S. M., Larson, C. L., Oakes, T. R., Holden, J. E., Perlman, S. B., et al. (1998). Metabolic rate in the right amygdala predicts negative affect in depressed patients. *NeuroReport, 9,* 3301–3307.

Alley, T. R., & Cunningham, M. R. (1991). Average faces are attractive, but very attractive faces are not average. *Psychological Science, 2,* 123–125.

Allgeier, E. R., & Wiederman, M. W. (1994). How useful is evolutionary psychology for understanding contemporary human sexual behavior? *Annual Review of Sex Research, 5,* 218–256.

Allport, G. W. (1937). *Personality: A psychological interpretation.* New York: Holt.

Apt, C., & Hurlbert, D. F. (1992). Motherhood and female sexuality beyond one year postpartum: A study of military wives. *Journal of Sex Education and Therapy, 18,* 104–114.

Bancroft, J. (1983). *Human sexuality and its problems.* Edinburgh: Churchill Livingstone.

Bancroft, J. (1989). *Human sexuality and its problem.* (2nd ed.). Edinburgh: Churchill Livingstone.

Bancroft, J. (1999). Central inhibition of sexual response in the male: A theoretical perspective. *Neuoscience and Biobehavioral Reviews, 23,* 763–784.

Bancroft, J. (2002). Biological factors in human sexuality. *The Journal of Sex Research, 39,* 15–21.

Bancroft, J., & Janssen, E. (2000). The dual control model of male sexual response: A theoretical approach to centrally mediated erectile dysfunction. *Neuroscience and Biobehavioral Reviews, 24,* 571–579.

Barber, N. (1995). The evolutionary psychology of physical attractiveness: Sexual selection and human morphology. *Ethnology and Sociobiology, 16*, 395–424.

Bailey, C. H., Dunne, M. P., & Martin, N. G. (2000). Genetic and environmental influences on sexual orientation and its correlates in an Australian twin sample. *Journal of Personality & Social Psychology, 78*, 524–536.

Beach, F. A. (1956). Characteristics of masculine "sex drive." In M. A. Jones (Ed.), *Nebraska Symposium on Motivation* (pp. 1–131). Lincoln, NE: University of Nebraska Press.

Bentham, J. (1789/1948). An introduction to the principles of morals and legislations. Oxford: Blackwell. (Originally published 1789)

Berenbaum, H., Raghaven, C., Le, H. N., Vernon, L., & Gomez, J. (1999). Disturbances in emotion. In D. Kahneman, E. Diener, & N. Schwartz (Eds.), *Well-being: The foundations of hedonic psychology* (pp. 267–287). New York: Russell Sage Foundation.

Berridge, K. C. (1999). Pleasure, pain, desire, and dread: Hidden core processes of emotion. In D. Kahneman, E. Diener, & N. Schwartz (Eds.), *Well-being: The foundations of hedonic psychology* (pp. 525–557). New York: Russell Sage Foundation.

Berscheid, E., & Reiss, H. T. (1998). Attraction and close relationships. In D. T. Gilbert (Ed.), *Handbook of social psychology* (pp. 193–281). New York: Random House.

Bertrocci, P. A. (1988). *The person and primary emotions.* New York: Springer-Verlag.

Bjornstorp, P. (1991). Adipose tissue distribution and function. *International Journal of Obesity, 15*, 67–81.

Bolig, R., Stein, P. J., & McKenny, P. C. (1984). The self-advertisements approach to dating: Male—female differences. *Family Relations, 33*, 587–592.

Brace, C. L. (1995). *The stages of human evolution* (5th ed.). Englewood Cliffs: Prentice-Hall.

Bradley, M. M., & Lang, P. J. (1994). Measuring emotion: The self-assessment manikin and the semantic differential. *Journal of Behavioral Therapy and Experimental Psychiatry, 25*, 49–59.

Bradman, N., & Thomas, M. (1998). Why Y? The Y chromosome in the study of human evolution, migration and prehistory. *Science Spectra*, 14, 14–23.

Bullough, V. L. (1964). *A history of prostitution.* New York: Basic Books.

Bullough, B., & Bullough, V. L. (1996). Female prostitution: Current research and changing interpretations. *Annual Review of Sex Research, 7*, 151–180.

Buss, D. M. (1984). Evolutionary biology and personality psychology. *American Psychologist, 39*, 1135–1147.

Buss, D. M. (1987). Sex differences in human mate selection criteria: An evolutionary perspective. In C. Crawford, D. Krebs, & M. Smith (Eds.), *Sociobiology and psychhology: Ideas, issues, and applications* (pp. 335–352). Hillside, NJ: Erlbaum.

Buss, D. M. (1989). Sex differences in human mate preferences: Evolutionary hypotheses tested in 37 cultures. *Behavioral and Brain Science, 12*, 1–49.

Buss, D. M. (1990). International preferences in selecting mates: A study of 37 cultures. *Journal of Cross Cultural Psychology, 21*, 5–47.

Buss, D. M. (1991). Evolutionary personality psychology. *Annual Review of Psychology, 42*, 459–491.

Buss, D. M. (1992). Mate preference mechanisms: Consequences for partner choice and intrasexual competition. In J. Barkow, L.Cosmides, & J. Tooby (Eds.), *The adapted mind: Evolutionary psychology and the generation of culture* (pp. 249–166). New York: Oxford University Press.

Buss, D. M. (1994). *The evolution of desire: Strategies of human mating.* New York: Basic Books.

Buss, D. M. (1998). Sexual strategies theory: Historical origins and current status. *The Journal of Sex Research, 35*, 19–31. Buss, D. M., & Kenrick, D. T. (1998). Evolutionary social psychology. In D. T. Gilbert, S. T. Fiske, & G.

Lindzey (Eds.), The *handbook of social psychology* (pp. 982–1026). New York: McGraw-Hill.

Buss, D. M., & Schmitt, D. P. (1993). Sexual strategies theory: An evolutionary perspective on human mating. *Psychological Review, 100,* 204–232.

Byrne, D. (1986). The study of sexual behavior as a multidisciplinary venture. In D.

Byrne, & K. K. Kelley (Eds.), *Alternative approaches to the study of sexual behavior* (pp. 1–12). London: Lawrence Erlbaum.

Cacioppo, J. T., & Gardner, W. L. (1999). Emotion. *Annual Review of Psychology, 50,* 191–214.

Cacioppo, J. T., Gardner, W. L., & Berntson, G. G. (1999). The affect system has parallel and integrative processing components: Form follows function. *Journal of Personality and Social Psychology, 76,* 839–855.

Cameron, C., Oskamp, S., & Sparks, W. (1977). Courtship American style—newspaper ads. *Family Coordinator, 26,* 27–30.

Campbell, J. (1988). The *power of myth.* New York: Doubleday.

Carver, C. S., & White, T. L. (1994). Behavioral inhibition, behavioral activation, and affective responses to impending reward and punishment: The BIS/BAS Scales. *Journal of Personality and Soiocial Psychology, 67,* 319–333.

Cosmides, L., Tooby, J., & Barkow, J. (1992). Introduction: Evolutionary psychology and conceptual integration. In J. Barkow, L.Cosmides, & J. Tooby, (Eds.), The *adapted mind: Evolutionary psychology and the generation of culture* (pp. 3–15). New York: Oxford University Press.

Cronbach, L. J., & Meehl, P. E. (1955). Construct validity in psychological tests. *Psychological Bulletin, 52,* 281–302.

Cunningham, M. R. (1986). Measuring the physical in physical attractiveness: Quasi-experiments on the sociobiology of female facial beauty. *Journal of Personality and Social Psycholology, 50,* 925–935.

Cunningham, M. R., Roberts, A. R., Barbie, A. P., Druen, P. B., & Wu, C. (1995). "There ideas of beauty are, on the whole, the same as ours": Consistency and variability in the cross-cultural perceptions of female physical attractiveness. *Journal of Personality and Social Psychology, 68,* 261–279.

Cuthbert, B. N., Schupp, H. T., Bradley, M. M., Birbaumer, N., & Lang, P. J. (2000). Brain potentials in affective picture processing: Covariation with autonomic arousal and affective report. *Biological Psychology, 52,* 95–111.

Dabbs, J. M., Jr. (1990). Salivary testosterone measurements: Reliability across hours, days, and weeks. *Physiology and Behavior, 48,* 83–86.

Dabbs, J. M., Jr., Campbell, B., Glaudue, B., Midgley, A., Navarro, M., Read, G., et al. (1995). Reliability of salivary testosterone measurements. *Enzymes and Protein Markers, 41,* 581–584.

Damasio, A. R. (1999). *The feeling of what happens: Body and emotion in the making of consciousness.* New York: Harcourt Brace.

Darwin, C. (1871). *The descent of man, and selection in relation to sex.* London: J. Murray.

Darwin, C. (1873/1965). *The expression of the emotions in man and animals.* Chicago: University of Chicago Press. (Original work published 1873)

Dashiell, J. F. (1928). *Fundamentals of objective psychology.* Boston, MA: Houghton Mifflin.

Davidson, R. J. (1984). Affect, cognition and hemispheric specialization. In C. E. Izard, J. Kagan, & R. Zajonc (Eds.), *Emotion, cognition and behavior* (pp. 320–365). New York: Cambridge University Press.

Davidson, R. J. (1992a). Anterior cerebral asymmetry and the nature of emotion. *Brain and Cognition, 20,* 125–151.

Davidson, R. J. (1992b). Emotion and affective style: Hemispheric substrates. *Psychological Science, 3,* 39–43.

Davidson, R. J. (1993). The neuropsychology of emotion and affective style. In M. Lewis, & J. M. Haviland (Eds.), *Handbook of emotions* (pp. 143–154). New York: The Guilford Press.

Davidson, R. J. (1994). Asymmetric brain function, affective style and psychopathology: The role of early experience and plasticity. *Development and Psychopathology, 6,* 741–757.

Davidson, R. J. (1998a). Affective style and affective disorders: Perspectives from affective neuroscience. *Cognition and Emotion, 12,* 307–330.

Davidson, R. J. (1998b). Anterior electrophysiological asymmetries, emotion and depression: Conceptual and methodological conundrums. *Psychophysiology, 35,* 607–614.

Davidson, R. J. (2000). Affective style, psychopathology and resilience: Brain mechanisms and plasticity. *American Psychologist, 55,* 1196–1214.

Davidson, R. J., Ekman, P., Saron, C., Senulis, J., & Friesen, W. V. (1990). Approach/withdrawal and cerebral asymmetry: Emotional expression and brain physiology I. *Journal of Personality and Social Psychology, 58,* 330–341.

Davidson, R. J., & Fox, N. A. (1982). Asymmetrical brain activity discriminates between positive versus negative affective stimuli in human infants. *Science, 218,* 1235–1237.

Davidson, R. J., & Fox, N. A. (1989). Frontal brain asymmetry predicts infants' response to maternal separation. *Journal of Abnormal Psychology, 98,* 127–131.

Davidson, R. J., & Irwin, W. (1999). The functional neuroanatomy of emotion and affective style. *Trends in Cognitive Science, 3,* 11–21.

Davidson, R. J., Jackson, D. C., & Kalin, N. H. (2000). Emotion, plasticity, context, and regulation: Perspectives from affective neuroscience. *Psychological Bulletin, 126,* 890–909.

Davidson, R. J., Pizzagalli, D., Nitschke, J. B., & Putnam, K. (2002). Depression: Perspectives from affective neuroscience. *Annual Review of Psychology, 32,* 545–574.

Davidson, R. J., & Tomarken, A. J. (1989). Laterality and emotion: An electrophysiological approach. In F. Boller & J. Grafman (Eds.), *Handbook of neuropsychology* (pp. 419–441). Amsterdam: Elsevier.

Davis, C. M., Yarber, W. L., Bauseman, R., Schreer, G., & Davis, S. L. (Eds.). (1999). *Handbook of sexuality-related measures.* Thousand Oaks, CA: Sage.

Depue, R. A., & Collins, P. F. (1999). Neurobiology of the structure of personality: Dopomine, facilitation of incentive motivation, and extraversion. *Behavioral and Brain Sciences, 22,* 491–569.

Depue, R. A., Luciana, M., Arbise, P., Collins, P., & Leon, A. (1994). Dopomine and the structure of personality: Relation of agonist-induced dopamine activity to positive emotionality. *Journal of Personality and Social Psychology, 67,* 485–498.

Dimberg, U., Elmehed, K., & Thurnberg, M. (2000). Unconscious facial reactions to emotional facial expressions. *Psychological Science, 11,* 86–89.

Ekman, P. (1992). An argument for basic emotions. *Cognition and Emotion, 6,* 169–200.

Ekman, P. (1993). Facial expression and emotion. *American Psychologist, 48,* 384–392.

Ekman, P., Davidson, R. J., & Friesen, W. V. (1990). The *Duchenne smile*: Emotional expression and brain physiology II. *Journal of Personality and Social Psychology, 58,* 342–353.

Ekman, P., & Friesen, W. V. (1978). *The Facial Action Coding System: A technique for the measurement of facial movement.* Palo Alto, CA: Consulting PsychologistsPress.

Ekman, P., & Friesen, W. V. (1982). Felt, false, and miserable smiles. *Journal of Nonverbal Behavior, 6,* 238–252.

Ellis, H. (1963). *Psychology of sex.* New York: New American Library of World Literature.

Erikson, E. H. (1950). *Childhood and society.* New York: Norton; 2nd ed.

Erikson,E. H. (1968). *Identity: Youth and crisis.* New York: Norton.

Evans, P. (1989). *Motivation and emotion.* London: Reutledge.

Everaerd, W., Laan, E., Both, & Spiering, M. (2001). Sexual motivation and desire. In W. Everaerd, E. Laan, & S. Both (Eds.), *Sexual appetite, desire and motivation: Energetics of the sexual system* (pp. 95–110). Amsterdam: Royal Netherlands Academy of Arts and Sciences.

Eysenck, H. J. (1967). *The biological basis of personality*. Springfield, IL: Charles C. Thomas.

Eysenck, H. J. (1976). The learning theory model of neurosis—a new approach. *Behavior Research and Therapy, 14*, 251–267.

Eysenck, H. J. (1997). Personality and experimental psychology: The unification of psychology and the possibility of a paradigm. *Journal of Personality and Social Psychology, 73*, 1224–1237.

Eysenck, H. J., & Eysenck, S. B. G. (1975). *Manual for the Eysenck Personality Questionnaire*. London: Hodder and Stoughton.

Filion, D. L., Dawson, M. E., & Schell, A. M. (1998). The psychological significance of human startle eyeblink modification: A review. *Biological Psychology, 47*, 1–43.

Fisher, W. W., Byrne, D., White, L. A., & Kelley, K. (1988). Erotophobia-erotophilia as a dimension of personality. *Journal of Sex Research, 25*, 123–151.

Ford, C. S., & Beach, F. A. (1951). *Patterns of sexual behavior*. New York: Harper.

Fortenbaugh, W. W. (1975). *Aristotle on emotions*. New York: Barnes and Noble.

Freud, A. (1946). The ego and the mechanisms of defence. New York: International Universities Press.

Freud, S. (1977). *Five lectures on psycho-analysis*. New York: Norton.

Freud, S. (1920/1965). *A general introduction to psychoanalysis*. New York: Washington Square Press.(Original work published 1920)

Frijda, N. H. (1986). *The emotions*. Cambridge: Cambridge University Press.

Furnham, A., Tan, T., & McManus, C. (1997). Waist-to-hip ratio and preferences for body shape: A replication and extension. *Personality and Individual Differences, 22,* 539–549.

Furnham, A., Hester, C., & Weir, C. (1990). Sex differences and the preferences for specific female body shapes. *Sex Roles, 22,* 743–754.

Gitter, A. G., Lomranz, J., & Saxe, L. (1982). Factors affecting perceived attractiveness of male physiques by Americans and Israeli students. *Journal of Social Psychology, 118,* 167–175.

Gitter, A. G., Lomranz, J., Saxe, L., & Bar-Tal, Y. (1983). Perception of female physique characteristics by American and Israeli students. *Journal of Social Psychology, 121,* 7–13.

Goldstein, K. (1939). *The organism.* New York: American Book. .

Grammar, K., & Thornhill, R. (1994). Facial attractiveness and sexual selection: The role of symmetry and averageness. *Journal of Comparative Psychology, 108,* 233–242.

Grant, S., London, E. D., Newlin, D. B., Villemagne, V. L., Xiang, L., Contoreggt, C., et al. (1996). Activation of memory circuits during cue-elicited cocaine craving. *Proceedings of the National Academy of Science, 93,* 12040–12045.

Gray, J. A. (1990). Brain systems that mediate both emotion and cognition. *Cognition and Emotion, 4,* 269–288.

Gray, J. A. (1994). The neuropsychology of the emotions: Framework for a taxonomy of psychiatric disorders. In *Emotions: Essays on emotion theory* (pp. 29–59). Hillsdale, NJ: Lawrence Erlbaum.

Guilford, J. P. (1950). *Fundamental statistics in psychology and education,* (2nd Ed.). New York: McGraw-Hill.

Hall, C. S., & Lindzey, G. (1957). *Theories of personality.* New York: John Wiley.

Hall, C. S., Lindzey, G., & Campbell, J. B. (1998). *Theories of personality,* (4th Ed.). New York: John Wiley.

Hamburg, D. A. (1963). Emotions in the perspective of human evolution. In P. H. Knapp (Ed.), *Expression of the emotions in man* (pp. 300–317). Madison, CT: International Universities Press.

Hardy, K.R. (1964). An appetitional theory of sexual motivation. *Psychological Review*, 1,1–18.

Harrison, A. A., & Saeed, L. (1977). Let's make a deal: Analysis of revelations and stipulations in lonely hearts advertisements. *Journal of Personality and Social Psychology, 35*, 257–264.

Henss, R. (1995). Waist-to-hip ratio and attractiveness. A replication and extension. *Personality and Individual Differences, 19*, 479–488.

Henss, R. (2000). Waist-to-hip ratio and attractiveness of the female figure. Evidence from photographic stimuli and methodological consideration. *Personality and Individual Differences, 28*, 501–513.

Higgins, E. T. (1997). Beyond pleasure and pain. *American Psychologist, 52*, 1280–1300.

Higgins, E. T., Grant, H., & Shah, J. (1999). Self-regulation and quality of life: Emotional and non-emotional life experiences. In D. Kahneman, E. Diener, & N. Schwartz (Eds.), *Well-being: The foundations of hedonic psychology* (pp. 244–266). New York: Russell Sage Foundation.

Hilgard, E. R., Atkinson, R. L., & Atkinson, R. C. (1979). *Introduction to psychology.* New York: Harcourt Brace Javanovich.

Hoebel, B. G., Rada, P. V., & Pothos, E. N. (1999). Neural systems for reinforcement and inhibition of behavior: Relevance to eating, addiction, and depression. In D. Kahneman, E. Diener, & N.Schwartz (Eds.), *Well-being: The foundations of hedonic psychology* (pp. 558–572). New York: Russell Sage Foundation.

Huffman, K. (2002). *Psychology in action.* New York: John Wiley.

Hulbert, D. F., Apt, C., & Rabehl, S. M. (1993). Key variables to understanding female sexual satisfaction: An examination of women in non distressed marriages. *Journal of Sex and Marital Therapy, 19*, 154–165.

Huskisson, E. C. (1974). Measurement of pain. *Lancet, 2*, 1127–1131.

Ito, T. A., & Cacioppo, J. T. (1999). The psychophysiology of utility appraisals. In D. Kahneman, E. Diener, & N. Schwartz (Eds.), *Well-being: The foundations of* hedonic psychology (pp. 470–488). New York: Russell Sage Foundation.

Izard, C. E. (1984). Emotion-cognition relationships and human development. In E.Izard, J. Kagan, & R. B. Zajonc (Eds.), *Emotion, cognition, and behavior* (pp. 17–37). New York: Cambridge University Press.

Izard, C. E. (1989). The structure and functions of emotions: Implications for cognition, motivation, and personality. In I. S. Cohen (Ed.), The G. Stanley Hall lecture series (Vol. 9, pp. 35–73). Washington, DC: American Psychological Association.

Izard, C. E. (1993). Four systems for emotion activation: Cognitive and non cognitive processes. *Psychological Review, 100*, 68–90.

Jackson, L. A. (1992). *Physical appearance and gender: Sociobiological and Sociocultural perspectives.* Albany: State University of New York Press.

James, W. (1890). *The principles of psychology.* New York: Holt.

Janssen, E. (1995). Provoking penile responses: Activation and inhibition of male genital response. Unpublished doctoral dissertation, University of Amsterdam, Amsterdam.

Janssen, E. (2002). Psychophysiological measurement of sexual arousal. In M. W. Wiederman, & B. E. Whitley, Jr. (Eds.), *Handbook for conducting research on human sexuality* (pp. 139–171). Mahwah, NJ: Lawrence Erlbaum.

Janssen, E., Everaerd, W., Spiering, M., & Janssen, J. (2000). Automatic processes and the appraisal of sexual stimuli: Toward an information processing model of sexual arousal. *The Journal of Sex Research, 37*, 8–23.

Janssen, E., Vorst, H., Finn, P., & Bancroft, J. (2002). The Sexual Inhibition (SIS) and Sexual Excitation (SES) Scales: I. Measuring sexual inhibition and excitation proneness in men. *The Journal of Sex Research, 39*, 114–126.

Jobling, M. A., & Tyler-Smith, C. Fathers and sons: The Y chromosome and human evolution. *Trends in Genetics, 11,* 449–456.

Johnston, B. S., & Franklin, M. (1993). Is Beauty in the eye of the beholder? *Ethololology and Sociobiology, 14,* 183–199.

Jones, D. (1995). Sexual selection, physical attractiveness, and facial neoteny. *Current Anthropology, 36.* 723–748.

Jung, C. G. (1953–1978). *Collected works.* In H. Read, M. Fordham, & G. Adler (Eds). Princeton: Princeton University Press.

Kahneman, D. (1999). Objective happiness. In D. Kahneman, E. Diener, & N. Schwartz (Eds.), *Well-being: The foundations of hedonic psychology* (pp. 3–25). New York: Russell Sage Foundation.

Kahneman, D., Diener, E., & Schwartz, N. (Eds.). (1999). *Well-being: The foundations of hedonic psychology.* New York: Russell Sage Foundation.

Kaplan, H. S. (1974). *The new sex therapy.* New York: Brunner/Mazel.

Kaplan, H. S. (1979). *Disorders of sexual desire and other new concepts and techniques in sex therapy.* New York: Simon and Schuster.

Kardiner, A. (1945). *The psychological frontiers of society.* New York: Columbia University Press.

Kennrick, D. T., & Keefe, R. C. (1992). Age preferences in mates reflect sex differences in human reproductive strategies. *Behavioral and Brain Sciences, 15,* 75–133.

Ketter, T. A., Andreason, P. J., George, M.S., Lee, C., Gill, D.S., Parekh, P. I., et al., (1996). Anterior paralimbic mediation of procaine-induced emotional and psychosensory experiences. *Archives of General Psychiaatry, 53,* 56–69.

Kinsey, A. C., Pomeroy, W. B., & Martin, C. E. (1948). *Sexual behavior in the human male.* Philadelphia, PA: W. B. Saunders.

Koch, M., Schmid, A., & Schnitzler, H. U. (1996). Pleasure-attenuation of the startle response is disrupted by 6-hydroxydopomine lesion of the nucleus accumbens. *Neuroreport, 7,* 1442–1446.

Koch, M., & Schnitzler, H. U. (1997). The acoustic startle response in rats-circuits mediating evocation, inhibition and potentiation. *Behavior and Brain Research, 89*, 35–49.

Kraft-Ebbing, R. (1945). *Psychopathia sexualis.* New York: Pioneer.

Lamiell, J. T. (1998). 'Nomethetic' and 'Idiographic': Contrasting Windelband's understanding with contemporary usage. *Theory and Psychology, 8*, 23–38.

Lange, C. (1885/1922). The emotions (I. A. Haupt, Trans.). Baltimore: Williams & Wilkins. (Original work published 1885)

Lang, P. J. (1994). The varieties of emotional experience: A meditation on James-Lange theory. *Psychological Review, 101*, 211–221.

Lang, P. J. (1995). The emotion probe: Studies of motivation and attention. *American Psychologist, 50*, 372–385.

Lang, P. J., Bradley, M. M., & Cuthbert, B. N. (1990). Emotion, attention, and the startle reflex. *Psychological Review, 97*, 377–395.

Lang, P. J., Bradley, M. M., & Cuthbert, B. N. (1998). Emotion, motivation, and anxiety: Brain mechanisms and psychophysiology. *Biological Psychiatry, 44*, 1248–1263.

Lang, P. J., Greenwald, M. K., Bradley, M. M., & Hamm, A. O. (1993). Looking at pictures: Affective, facial, visceral, and behavioral reactions. *Psychophysiology, 30*, 261–273.

Langlois, J.H., Kalaknis, L., Rubenstein, A. J., Larson, A., H., Hallam, M., & Smoot, M. (2000). Maxims or myths of beauty? A meta-analytic and theoretical review. *Psychological Bulletin, 126*, 390–423.

Langlois, J. H., & Roggman, L. A. (1990). Attractive faces are only average. *Psychological Science, 1*, 115–121.

Larsen, R. J., & Diener, E. (1987). Emotional response intensity as an individual difference characteristic. *Journal of Research in Personality*, 21, 1–30.

Lazarus, R. S. (1984). On the primacy of cognition. *American Psychologist, 39*, 124–129.

LeDoux, J. E. (1992). Emotion and the limbic system concept. *Concepts in Neuroscience, 2,* 169–199.

LeDoux, J. E. (1993). Emotional networks in the brain. In M. Lewis, & J. M.Haviland (Eds.), *Handbook of emotions* (pp. 109–118). New York: The Guilford Press.

LeDoux, J. E. (1995). Emotion: Clues from the brain. *Annual Review of Psychology, 45,* 209.-235.

LeDoux, J. E. (1996). *The emotional brain.* New York: Simon and Schuster.

LeDoux, J. E. (2000). Emotion circuits in the brain. *Annual Review of Neuroscience, 23* 155–184.

Lichtenberg, J.D. (1989). *Psychoanalysis and motivation.* New Jersey: The Analytic Press.

Livshits, G., & Kobliansky, E. (1991). Fluctuating asymmetry as a possible measure of developmental homeostasis in humans: A review. *Human Biology, 63,* 441–466.

Manning, J. T., Scutt, D., Whitehouse, G. H. & Leinster, S. J. (1997). Breast asymmetry and phenotypic quality in women. *Evolutionary Human Behavior, 18,* 223–236.

Maslow, A. H. (1954). *Motivation and personality.* New York: Harper and Row (2nd ed., 1970).

Masters, W. H., & Johnson, V. E. (1966). *Human sexual response.* Boston, MA: Little Brown.

Masters W. H., & Johnson, V. E. (1970). *Human sexual inadequacy.* Boston, MA: Little Brown.

Mazur, A., & Booth, A. (1998). Testosterone and dominance in men. *Behavioral and Brain Sciences, 21,* 353–397.

Møller, A. P., Soler, M., & Thornhill, R. (1995). Breast asymmetry, sexual selection and human reproductive success. *Ethology and Sociobiology, 16,* 207–219.

Murray, H. A., Barrett, W. G., & Homburger, E. (1938). *Explorations in personality.* New York: Oxford University Press.

Ness, R. M. (1990). Evolutionary explanations of emotions. *Human Nature, 1,* 261–289.

Öhman, A., & Mineka, S. (2000). Fears, phobias, and preparedness: Toward an evolved module of fear and fear learning. *Psychological Review, 108,* 483–522.

Okami, P., & Shakelford, T. K. (2001). Human sex differences in sexual psychology and behavior. *Annual Review of Sex Research, 12,* 186–241.

Peterson, J. R. (1999). *The Century of Sex.* New York: Grove Press.

Price, D. D., McGrath, P. A., Rabie, A., & Buckinggham, B. (1983). *Pain, 17,* 45–56.

Rabkin, J.G., Rabkin, R., & Wagner, G. (1995). Testosterone replacement therapy in HIV illness. *General Hospital Psychiatry, 17,* 37–42.

Regan, P. C., & Berscheid, E. (1999). *Lust: What we know about human sexual desire.* Thousand Oaks, CA: Sage.

Reich, W. (1973). *The function of the orgasm.* New York: Noonday Press.

Rogers, C. R. (1961). *On becoming a person.* Boston: Houghton Mifflin.

Rolls, E. T. (1990). A theory of emotion, and its application to understanding the neural basis of emotion. *Cognition and Emotion, 4,* 161–190.

Rosen, R. C., & Beck, J. G. (1988). *Patterns of sexual arousal.* New York: The Guilford Press.

Rosen, J. B., & Schulkin, J. (1998). From normal fear to pathological anxiety. *Psychological Review, 105,* 325–350.

Rouseau, J. J. (1762–1979). *Émile.* New York: Basic Books. (Original work published 1762)

Rowland, D. L. (1999), Issues in the laboratory study of human sexual response. *The Journal of Sex Research, 36,* 3–15.

Ryan, R. M., & Deci, E. L. (2001). On happiness and human potentials: A review of research on hedonic and eudaimonic well-being. *Annual Review of Psychology, 52*, 141–166.

Sachs, B. D. (2000). Contextual approaches to the physiology and classification of erectile function, erectile dysfunction, and sexual arousal. *Neuroscience and Biobehavioral Reviews, 24*, 541–560.

Schnierla, T. (1959). An evolutionary and developmental theory of biphasic processes underlying approach and withdrawal. In M. Jones (Ed.), *Nebraska Symposium on Motivation*. Lincoln: University of Nebraska Press.

Shea, B. J. (1989). Heterochrony in human evolution: The case for neoteny reconsidered. *Yearbook of Physical Anthropology, 32*, 69–101.

Shizgal, P. (1999). On the neural computation of utility: Implications from studies of brain stimulation reward. In D. Kahneman, E.Diener, & N. Schwartz (Eds.), *Well-being: The foundations of hedonic psychology* (pp. 500–524). New York: Russell Sage Foundation.

Siegelman, M. (1972 a). Adjustment of homosexual and heterosexual women. *British Journal of Psychiatry, 120*, 477–481.

Siegelman, M. (1972 b). Adjustment of male homosexuals and heterosexuals. *Archives of Sexual Behavior, 2*, 9–25.

Siegelman, M. (1974 a). Parental background of homosexual and heterosexual women. *British Journal of Psychiatry, 124*, 14–21.

Siegelman, M. (1974 b). Parental background of male homosexuals and heterosexuals. *Archives of Sexual Behavior, 3*, 3–18.

Siegelman, M. (1978). Psychological adjustment of homosexual and heterosexual men: A cross-national replication. *Archives of Sexual Behavior, 7*, 1–11.

Siegelman, M. (1979). Adjustment of homosexual and heterosexual women: A cross-national replication. *Archives of Sexual Behavior, 8*, 121–125.

Siegelman, M. (1981a). Parental background of homosexual and heterosexual women: A cross-national replication. *Archives of Sexual Behavior, 10*, 369–375.

Siegelman, M. (1981b). Parental backgrounds of homosexual and heterosexual men: A cross-national replication. *Archives of Sexual Behavior, 10,* 505–513.

Siegelman, M. Kinsey and others: Empirical input. In L. Diamant (Ed.) Male and female homosexuality (pp. 33–79). Washington: Hemisphere Publishing Corporation.

Singer, B., & Toates, F. (1987). Sexual motivation. *The Journal of Sex Research, 4,* 481–501.

Singh, D. (1993a). Adaptive significance of female physical attractiveness: Role of waist-to-hip ratio. *Journal of Personality and Social Psychology, 65,* 293–307.

Singh, D. (1993b). Body shape and women's attractiveness: The critical role of waste-to-hip ratio. *Human Nature, 4,* 297–321. .

Singh, D. (1994a). Ideal female body shape: The role of body weight and Waist-to-Hip ratio. *International Journal of Eating Disorders, 16,* 283–288.

Singh, D. (1994b). Is thin really beautiful and good? Relationship between waist-to-hip ratio (WHR) and female attractiveness. *Personality and Individual Differences, 16,* 123–132.

Singh, D. (1995). Female health, attractiveness, and desirability for relationships: Role of breast asymmetry and waist-to-hip ratio. *Ethology and Sociobiology, 16,* 465–481.

Skinner, B. F. (1953). *Science and human behavior.* New York: Macmillan.

Smith, C. A., & Ellsworth, P. C. (1985). Patterns of cognitive appraisal. *Journal of Personality and Social Psychology, 48,* 813–838.

Smith, C. A., & Ellsworth, P. C. (1987). Patterns of appraisal and emotion related to taking an exam. *Journal of Personality and Social Psychology, 52,* 475–488.

Stellar, J. R., & Stellar, E. (1985). *The neurobiology of motivation and reward.* New York: Springer-Verlag.

Stephan, W. G. (1992). Sexual motivation, patriarchy and compatibility. *Behavioral and Brain Science, 15,* 112.

Stoléru, S., Grégoire, M. C., Gérard, D., Decety, J., Lafarge, E., Cinotti, L., et al. (1999). Neuroanatomical correlates of visually evoked sexual arousal in human males. *Archives of Sexual Behavior, 28,* 1–21.

Sutton, S. K., & Davidson, R. J. (1997). Prefrontal brain asymmetry: A biological substrate of the behavioral approach and inhibition systems. *Psychological Science, 8,* 204–210.

Sutton, S. K., Ward, R. T., Larson, C. L., Holden, J. E., Perlman, S. B., & Davidson, R. J. (1997). Asymmetry in prefrontal glucose metabolism during appetitive and aversive emotional states: An FDG-PET study. *Psychophysiology, 34,* S89.

Symons, D. (1979). *The evolution of human sexuality.* New York: Oxford University Press.

Symons, D. (1992). On the use and misuse of Darwinism in the study of human behavior. In J. Barkow, L. Cosmedes, & J. Tooby. (Eds.), *The adapted mind: Evolutionary psychology and the generation of culture* (pp.137–159). New York: Oxford University Press.

Symons, D. (1995). Beauty is in the adaptation of the beholder: The evolutionary psychology of human female sexual attractiveness. In P. R. Abramson & S. D. Pinkerton (Eds.), *Sexual nature sexual culture* (pp. 80–118). Chicago: University of Chicago Press.

Tassinary, L. G., & Cacioppo, J. T. (1992). Unobservable facial action emotions. *Psychological Science, 3,* 28–33.

Thorndike, E. L. (1932). *The psychology of wants, interests, and attitudes.* New York: Appleton-Century-Crofts.

Thornhill, R., & Gangestad, S. W. (1994). Fluctuating asymmetry and human sexual behavior. *Psychological Science, 5,* 297–302.

Thornhill, R., & Gangstad, S. W. (1995). Human facial beauty: Averageness, symmetry and parasite resistance. *Human Nature, 4,* 237–269.

Thornhill, R., & Grammar, K. (1999). The body and face of woman: One ornament that signals quality? *Evolution and Human Behavior, 20*, 105–120.

Titchner, E. B. (1908). *Lectures on elementary psychology of feeling and attention.* New York: Macmillan.

Tolman, E. C. (1932). *Purposive behavior in animals and man.* New York: Century.

Tomarkin, A. J., Davidson, R. J., Wheeler, R. E., & Doss, R. C. (1992). Individual differences in anterior brain asymmetry and fundamental dimensions of emotion. *Journal of Personality and Social Psychology, 62*, 676–686.

Tomarkin, A. J., Davidson, R. J., Wheeler, R. W., & Kinney, L. (1992). Psychometric properties of resting anterior EEG asymmetry: Temporal stability and internal consistency. *Psychophysiology, 29*, 575–592.

Tomarkin, A. J., & Keener, A. D. (1998). Frontal brain asymmetry and depression: A self-regulatory perspective. *Cognition and Emotion, 12*, 387–420.

Tooby, J., & Cosmides. L. (1992). The psychological foundation of culture. In J. Barkow, L. Cosmides, & J. Tooby (Eds.), *The adapted mind: Evolutionary psychology and the generation of culture* (pp. 19–136). New York: Oxford University Press.

Tovée, M.J., & Cornelissen, P. L. (1999). The mystery of female beauty. *Nature, 399*, 215–216.

Tovée, M. J., & Cornelissen, P. L. (2001). Female and male perceptions of female physical attractiveness in front-view and profile. *British Journal of Psychology, 92*. 391–402.

Tovée, M. J., Mason, M., Emery, J. L., McClusky, S. E., & Cohen-Tovee, E. M. (1997). Supermodels: Stick insects or hourglass. *Lancet, 350*, 1474–1475.

Tovée, M. J., Reinhardt, S., Emery, J. L., & Cornelissen, P. L. (1998). Optimal BMI and maximum sexual attractiveness. *Lancet, 352*, 548.

Tovée, M. J., Tasker, K., & Benson, P. J. (2000). Is symmetry a visual cue to attractiveness in the human female body? *Evolution and Human Behavior, 21*, 191–200.

Tucker, D. M., & Williamson, P. A. (1984). Asymmetric neural control systems in human self-regulation. *Psychological Review, 91*, 185–215.

Trivers, R. (1972). Parental investment and sexual selection. In B. Campbell (Ed.), *Sexual selection and the descent of man* (pp. 136–179). New York: Aldine de Gruzter.

Valenstein, E. S. (1976). The interpretation of behavior evoked by brain stimulation. In A.Wauquier & E. T. Rolls (Eds.), *Brain-stimulation reward* (pp. 557–575). New York: Elsevier.

Volkow, N. D., Wang, G. J., & Fowler, J. S. (1997). Imaging studies of cocaine in the human brain and studies of the cocaine addict. *Annals of the New York Academy of Sciences, 820*, 41–45.

Wass, P., Waldenstrom, U., Rossner, S., & Hellberg, D. (1997). An android body fat distribution in females impairs the pregnancy rate of in-vitro fertilization-embryo transfer. *Human Reproduction, 12*, 2057–2060.

Watson, D., Clark, L. A., & Tellegen, A. (1988). Development and validation of brief measures of positive and negative affect: The PANAS scales. *Journal of Personality and Soicial Psychology, 54*, 1963–1070.

Watson, D., Wiese, D., Vaidya, J., & Tellegen, A. (1999). The two general activation systems of affect: Structural findings, evolutionary considerations, and psychobiological evidence. *Journal of Personality and Social Psychology, 70*, 820–838.

Webster's third new international dictionary of the English language unabridged. (1986). Springfield, MA: Merriam-Webster.

Weis, D. L. The use of theory in sexuality research. (1998). *The Journal of Sex Research, 35*, 1–9.

Weiss, D. L. (2002). Another stab at sexual theory [Review of the book The role of theory in sex research]. *The Journal of Sex Research, 39*, 158–160.

Whalen, R. E (1966). Sexual motivation. *Psychological Review, 2*, 151–163.

Williams, G. C. (1975). *Sex and evolution.* Princeton, NJ: Princeton University Press.

Wise, R. A. (1982). Common neural basis of brain stimulation reward, drug reward, and food reward. In B. G. Hoebel & D. Novin (Eds.), *The neural basis of feeding and reward* (pp. 445–454). Brunswick ME: Haer Institute

Wise, R. A. (1996). Addictive drugs and brain stimulation reward. *Annual Review of Neuroscience, 19*, 319–340.

Yeomans, J. S. (1989). Two substrates for medial forebrain bundle self-stimulation: Myelinated axons and dopamine axons. *Neuroscience and Biobehavioral Review, 13*, 91–98.

Zaadstra, B. M., Seidell, J. C., Van Noord, P. A. H., te Velde, E. R., Habbema, J. D. F., Vrieswijk, B., & Karbaat, J. (1993). Fat and female fecundity: Prospective study of effect of body fat distribution on conception rates. *British Medical Journal, 306*, 484–487.

Zajonc, R. B. (1980). Feeling and thinking: Preferences need no inferences. *American Psychologist, 35*, 151–175.

Zajonc, R. B. (1984). On the primacy of affect. *American Psychologist, 39*, 117–123.

Zajonc, R. B. (1998). Emotions. In D. T. Gilbert, S. T. Fisk, & G. Lindzey (Eds.), *The handbook of social psychology* (pp. 591–632). Vol. 2 (4th ed.) (pp. 591–632). Boston, MA: McGraw-Hill.

Zuckerman, M. (1984). Sensation seeking: A comparative approach to a human trait. *Behavioral and Brain Sciences, 7*, 413–471.

Zuckerman, M. (1987). A critical look at three arousal constructs in personality theories: Optimal level of arousal, strength of the nervous system, and sensitivities to signals of reward and punishment. In J. Strelau, & H. J. Eysenck (Eds.), *Personality dimensions and arousal* (pp. 217–231). New York: Plenum.

Zuckerman, M. (1991). *Psychobiology of personality.* Cambridge: Cambridge University Press.

Zuckerman, M. (1994). *Behavioral expression and biosocial bases of sensation seeking.* New York: Cambridge University Pres

Zuckerman, M., & Kuhlman, D. M. (2000). Personality and risk-taking: Common biosocial factors. *Journal of Personality, 68*, 999–1029.

About the Author

Professor emeritus The City College of New York. Research associate Harvard University. New York State licensed psychologist. Member of The International Academy of Sex Research and the Society for the Scientific Study of Sexuality. Taught undergraduate courses in human sexuality and graduate courses in sex therapy and sexual dysfunctions at Mercy College in New York.

978-0-595-32395-1
0-595-32395-2

www.ingramcontent.com/pod-product-compliance
Lightning Source LLC
Chambersburg PA
CBHW061309280526
45784CB00002B/938

* 9 7 8 0 5 9 5 3 2 3 9 5 1 *